中国思想文化术语多语种对外翻译
标准化建设项目成果
CHINESE THINKING AND CULTURE
MULTILINGUAL TERMINOLOGY DATABASE

中华源·河南故事
CHINESE CIVILIZATION
Stories from Henan

"人工天河"红旗渠
MAN-MADE RIVER — HONGQIQU CANAL

主编 李向前
EDITOR-IN-CHIEF: LI XIANGQIAN

河南大学出版社
HENAN UNIVERSITY PRESS
·郑州·

图书在版编目（CIP）数据

中华源·河南故事."人工天河"红旗渠 / 李向前主编. -- 郑州：河南大学出版社，2019.6（2021.12重印）

ISBN 978-7-5649-2691-5

Ⅰ. ①中… Ⅱ. ①李… Ⅲ. ①地方文化－河南－通俗读物②红旗渠－介绍 Ⅳ. ①G127.61-49②U621

中国版本图书馆CIP数据核字（2019）第093280号

责任编辑	郑　鑫　林方丽
责任校对	田丽贞
封面设计	翟淼淼
出版发行	河南大学出版社
	地址：郑州市郑东新区商务外环中华大厦2401号　邮编：450046
	电话：0371-86059701（营销部）　0371-86059753（大众读物分公司）
	网址：hupress.henu.edu.cn
排　版	河南博雅彩印有限公司
印　刷	河南博雅彩印有限公司
版　次	2020年1月第1版
印　次	2021年12月第2次印刷
开　本	710 mm×1010 mm 1/16
印　张	10.5
字　数	145千
定　价	58.50元

版权所有，侵权必究

本书如有印装质量问题，请与河南大学出版社营销部联系调换。

"中华源·河南故事"系列丛书编委会

顾　　问　　黄友义　杨　平　范大祺
名誉主任　　穆为民　何金平
主　　任　　付　静
副 主 任　　陈志伟　刁玉华　李向前　李　镇　梁留科
　　　　　　刘金锋　孔留安　史永庆　许二平　万正峰
　　　　　　杨建伟　杨玮斌　王建修　王自文　张改平
　　　　　　张松文　赵卫东

主　　编　　付　静
执行主编　　杨玮斌
编　　委　　陈　玮　丁　锐　高　阳　徐恒振

中华源：河南故事·"人工天河"红旗渠

主　　编　　李向前
副 主 编　　王宝玉　柳红英　党兰玲（英文）
中文撰稿　　申伏生
英文译者　　党兰玲　李胜机　雷冬雪　李慧敏　刘全勇
英文审校　　Cody Turner（美）

The Editorial Committee
Chinese Civilization
Stories from Henan

Consultants	Huang Youyi Yang Ping Fan Daqi
Honorary Directors	Mu Weimin He Jinping
Director	Fu Jing
Deputy Directors	Chen Zhiwei Diao Yuhua Li Xiangqian Li Zhen
	Liang Liuke Liu Jinfeng Kong Liu'an Shi Yongqing
	Xu Erping Wan Zhengfeng Yang Jianwei
	Yang Weibin Wang Jianxiu Wang Ziwen
	Zhang Gaiping Zhang Songwen Zhao Weidong

Chief Editor	Fu Jing
Executive Chief Editor	Yang Weibin
Editors	Chen Wei Ding Rui Gao Yang Xu Hengzhen

Chinese Civilization
Stories from Henan
Man-made River — Hongqiqu Canal

Editor-in-Chief	Li Xiangqian
Associate Editors-in-Chief (English Text)	Wang Baoyu Liu Hongying Dang Lanling
Writer	Shen Fusheng
Translators	Dang Lanling Li Shengji Lei Dongxue
	Li Huimin Liu Quanyong
Translation Proofreader	Cody Turner(America)

总 序

中国是世界四大文明古国之一，也是世界上唯一的古代文明传统未曾中断的国家。河南省地处中国中东部，是中华文明和中华民族的重要发祥地，在中国五千年的文明史上，河南作为国家政治、经济、文化的中心就长达三千多年。从某种意义上讲，一部河南史就是半部中国史。这里是中华人文始祖黄帝的故乡，是古丝绸之路的东方起点，是少林功夫和陈氏太极的发源地，这里创建了中国历史上最早的都城，镌刻了中国最古老的文字，诞生了中国最初的商业文明。

伴随着新时代的荣光，河南经济社会发展迅速，人民生活水平显著提升，这是自力更生、艰苦奋斗的历史结果，也是对外开放带来的益处。河南经济社会的发展、人民生活方式的改变都植根于深层次的文化积淀。为了让世界更多地了解河南，让河南更好地走向世界，2018年以来，河南省外事办认真研析了这片古老土地上的历史文化资源和时代风貌，组织各领域权威专家学者，编译了"中华源·河南故事"中外文系列丛书，选取少林功夫、太极拳、中医、汉字、文物、焦裕禄、红旗渠、丝绸之路、古都、农业、手工艺等多个主题，力图以故事的方式向世界展现一个立体、全面、真实的河南。

当今世界，人类文明无论在物质还是精神方面都取得了巨大进步，特别是物质的极大丰富是古代世界完全不能想象的。同时，当代人类也面临着许多突出的难题，比如，贫富差距持续扩大，物欲追求奢华无度，个人主义恶性膨胀，社会诚信不断消减，伦理道德每况愈下，人与自然关系日趋紧张，等等。要解决这些难题，不仅需要运用人类今天发现和发展的智慧和力量，而且需要运用人类历史上积累和储存的智慧和力量。河南历史文化底蕴深厚、包容性强，在今天仍极具现实意义。中原文化蕴含的思想智慧有助于修身养性，推动人类社会进步发展，焦裕禄精神、红旗渠精神所体现的为民爱民、艰苦奋斗的价值取向是构建人类命运共同体的力量源泉。我们期待与读者们一起从河南故事中汲取更多的智慧和力量，共同创造更加美好的未来。

Series Foreword

China is one of the four ancient civilizations in the world, and is also the only country in the world where the ancient civilization has not been interrupted. Located in east-central China, Henan province is an important cradle for the Chinese nation and the Chinese civilization. In the course of the five thousand years of Chinese history, for more than three thousand years it served as the political, economic and cultural center of the country and therefore, as generally accepted, represents half of the history of China. Henan is the native place of Yellow Emperor, the cradle of Chinese culture, the starting point of the ancient Silk Road in the east, and the birthplace of Shaolin Kungfu and Chen-style Taijiquan—typical examples of the world-renowned Chinese martial arts. It was here that the earliest capital city in China was founded, the oldest Chinese characters engraved, and the earliest commerce took shape.

In the new era, Henan has witnessed rapid growth in its economy and remarkable improvement of people's living conditions, owing to the national reform and opening-up policy and unremitting endeavoring of the people. Modern economic achievements and social development as well as the changes of way of life could be traced back to its traditional values and cultural heritages. To enable people from other countries to understand Henan, and let the province integrate more efficiently into the world development, the Foreign Affairs Office of the People's Government of Henan province, has organized teams of authoritative experts and scholars in relevant fields to compile this *Chinese Civilization: Stories from Henan* in Chinese and other foreign languages since 2018, by crystallizing the excellence of traditions and outstanding features of modern development. The book series include *Shaolin Kungfu, Taijiquan, Traditional Chinese Medicine, Chinese Characters, Cultural Heritage, A Model Official — Jiao Yulu, Man-made River — Hongqiqu Canal, the Silk*

Road, *Ancient Chinese Capitals*, *Handicraft* and *Feeding the People — Agriculture*, etc, attempting to present a panoramic picture of the province.

In today's world, human civilization has made great progress in both material accumulation and cultural and ethical advancement, and the great abundance of materials today, especially, is beyond the imagination of the ancient people. At the same time, however, modern people are also confronted with a lot of problems, such as the widening gap between the rich and the poor, the indulgence in pursuit of luxury and extravagance, the undesirable extension of individualism, the decline of social integrity, and the increasing tension between man and nature. To solve these problems, we need to draw on the wisdom and powers developed today as well as those accumulated in the past. Henan is endowed with a rich historical and cultural heritage characterized by its inclusiveness, and such a heritage remains significant today. The intelligence and wisdom in Henan culture are conducive to self-cultivation and to the promotion of social development. The spirit of serving the people and relentless struggle, as embodied in *Jiao Yulu* and *Hongqiqu Canal*, provides source of strength for building a community with a shared future for mankind. It is our hope that, wisdom and strength from Henan stories, could lead us to a shared brilliant future.

前 言

从约2亿1千万年前开始到6500万年前，地球上发生了被称为燕山运动的大地构造运动。在中国的华北地区，地壳因为受到强有力的挤压，褶皱隆起，形成了东北—西南走向，绵延400余公里的太行山脉。太行山是我国陆地地势第二三级阶梯的分界线，同时也是华北平原与黄土高原的天然界线。习惯上人们把太行山分为三段，在山西省境内的部分称为西太行，在河北省境内的部分称为北太行，位于河南省境内的部分称为南太行。林县（今林州市）位于南太行的东麓、河南省西北角，处在山西、河北、河南三省交界处，1994年，林县撤县设市，以古名林州命名，改名为林州市（县级）。

受华北平原地层断裂下沉的拖拽，林州境内地质构造活动强烈，以断裂构造为主，沿山脊走向的大断裂十分发育。林州境内断层较多，大多属于正断层。最大的断层位于林州盆地的西部并延长到北部，长约35公里，断层面倾向东，倾角50°~80°，垂直断距约1000米。除此之外，林州境内还有4处较大的断层和众多小断层。由于林州境内大小30多条断层交错出现，加之境内广泛分布着石灰岩，多裂隙、溶洞，使得地表水流失严重，林州也因此成为资源性缺水地区。

林州属于暖温带大陆性季风气候，四季分明，夏季高温多雨，冬季寒冷干燥。林州年平均降水量约为672.1mm，降水量季节分配不均，每年七、八两个月的降水量占60%~70%，其他10个月只占全年降水量的30%~40%。林州多年平均蒸发量为1513.5mm，年蒸发量是年降水量的2倍多。蒸发旺盛，降水不足，这也是造成林州水资源短缺的一个重要原因。

太行山作为河南省与山西省的界山，其山脊多为地表分水岭。林州位于分水岭的东侧，汇水面积小，境内河流距离源头较近，流量小，当地河流（除过境的漳河外）平时干涸断流，汛期水势猛涨，地表水资源可利用量较小。

林州大气降水较少，地表水资源可利用量较小，千山万壑的地貌使降水与地表水入渗条件差，地下断层大面积分布无稳定的含水层，在有隔水层地方，地下水埋藏较深，开采相当困难。在早期，干旱缺水成为这个地区的常态，严重制约着林州人民的生存和发展。

在中国古老的神话传说中，天宫的仙子织女与人间的穷小子牛郎相爱了。这段严重违反天条的恩爱姻缘，惹恼了天宫的女主管王母娘娘。她拔下头上的金簪，在天空中划出了一条波涛滚滚的银河，拆散了这对天地姻缘。正是这个神话传说，中国人的语境中就有了"天河"这个概念。

人间的干旱如同一柄锋利的达摩克利斯剑，高悬在每一个林州人头上，高悬在这个古老县邑的生命线上。干渴的人们仰望苍天，想象着天河里该有多少水呀，都流向了哪里？要是流到太行山上、流向林州该多好啊！

牛郎织女的神话在林州人民中代代口耳相传，每一个听故事的孩子都恨王母娘娘，谁都怕有一个像王母娘娘那样的外婆。等到他们长大了，倒是喜欢起王母娘娘了，不是喜欢这个外婆，而是喜欢她手里那枚轻轻一划就划出一条银河的金簪。要是咱们也有那样一枚金簪，在太行山上一划，划出一条银河，咱林州不就不缺水了么？怎么才能得到王母娘娘的金簪呢？

多少代的期盼，多少辈的等待，等待着找到一枚王母娘娘的金簪，在太行山上一划，天上银河落太行，击退悬在头上的那把干旱的达摩克利斯剑。

王母娘娘是不会为林州人着想的，一个天上的织女下嫁，她都忍无可忍，怎能允许林州人涉足天上的生活呢？但她那轻轻的一划，启发林州人敢于向天神夺过来金簪，擘画出一条人工河流。

　　历史的车轮驶入1960年，林州人发现金簪就在自己手中，自己就是神话里的王母娘娘。要想过上神仙般的生活只有自力更生、艰苦奋斗，才能使手中的铁锤钢钎百炼成金簪。于是，千万人齐心协力一划，裂石穿山，划破了太行山苍老荒凉的皮肤，断漳河于峡谷，引河水于断崖，远在山那边的漳河水从空中流入了林州，从此中国的地图上增添了一条蓝色曲线，太行山上诞生了一条人工天河。

Preface

From about 210 million years ago to 65 million years ago, a geotectonic movement known as the Yanshan Movement took place on the earth. In North China, the crust was strongly squeezed and upheaved, which formed the Taihang Mountains, stretching from the northeast to the southwest over 400 kilometers. The Taihang Mountains is the dividing line between the second and third steps of China's land topography, and it is also the natural boundary between the North China Plain and the Loess Plateau. Customarily, the Taihang Mountains is divided into three sections, namely, the West Taihang in Shanxi Province, the North Taihang in Hebei Province and the South Taihang in Henan Province. Linxian County (now Linzhou City), located at the eastern foot of the South Taihang and in the northwest of Henan Province, is at the junction of Shanxi, Hebei and Henan provinces. In 1994, Linxian County was renamed Linzhou City after the ancient name Linzhou.

Due to the fault and subsidence of the stratum in the North China Plain, the geological tectonic activity in Linzhou is strong, and based mainly on the fault structure, the large fault along the ridge is well developed. There are many faults in Linzhou, most of which belong to normal faults. The largest fault, about 35 kilometers long, is located in the western part of the Linzhou Basin and extends to the north. The fault plane inclines eastward, with the dip angle of $50°~80°$ and the vertical fault distance about 1,000 meters. In addition, there are four other large faults and many small faults in Linzhou. Due to the interlacing of more than 30 faults in Linzhou, and the wide distribution of limestone, together with numerous fissures and karst caves, the surface water loss is very serious, causing Linzhou to be a water shortage area.

Linzhou belongs to the warm temperate continental monsoon climate with four distinct seasons, hot and rainy in summer, and cold and dry in winter. The average annual precipitation in Linzhou is about 672.1 mm. The precipitation season is unevenly distributed. The precipitation in July and August accounts for 60%~70%, and only 30~40% of the annual precipitation for 10 months in spring, autumn and winter. The average annual evaporation of Linzhou is 1,513.5 mm, more than twice that of the precipitation. The strong evaporation and insufficient precipitation contributes chiefly to the shortage of water resources in Linzhou.

As a boundary between Henan Province and Shanxi Province, the ridges of the Taihang Mountains are mostly the watersheds of the earth's surface. Linzhou is located on the east of the watershed. The catchment area is small. The rivers in the territory are close to the sources, with small water flow. The local rivers(except the Zhanghe River) that passes through are usually dry, but full of water during the flood season. Therefore, the surface water resources are less available.

Linzhou has less atmospheric precipitation and less available surface water resources, and the landforms of the mountains and valleys make it hard for the precipitation and surface water to infiltrate. The underground faults are distributed in large areas without stable aquifers and the groundwater is buried deep and difficult to exploit. In the early days, drought and water shortage became the normal state of this region, which seriously restricted the survival and development of the people of Linzhou.

In ancient Chinese myths, the celestial fairy Zhinü fell in love with the poor boy Niulang. The conjugal love, which was a serious violation of the heaven's law, annoyed the Queen Mother, the female ruler in the heavenly palace. She pulled a gold hairpin off her hair and drew a rolling Milky Way in the sky, breaking up the marriage between heaven and earth. It is this myth that gives the Chinese context the concept of "Tianhe", namely the Heavenly River.

Drought was like a sharp sword of Damocles, hanging over the people of Linzhou, and over the life line of this ancient county. The thirsty people looked up at the sky, imagining how much water there was in the Heavenly River. They wondered how nice it would be if it could flow to the Taihang Mountains and to Linzhou!

The myth of Niulang and Zhinü has been passed down from generation to generation among the people of Linzhou. Every child who heard the tale hated the Queen Mother very much and was afraid of having a grandmother like her. When they grew up, they liked the Queen Mother, just because of her gold hairpin that could scribe a Heavenly River with a slight stroke. If they had had such a gold hairpin, they could have drawn a river in the Taihang Mountains, thus the people of Linzhou would no longer be in short of water. How could they get the gold hairpin from the Queen Mother?

How many generations had been expecting and waiting to find the Queen Mother's gold hairpin, so that it could draw a river on the Taihang Mountains to repel the sword of Damocles hanging over the head?

The Queen Mother would never think of the Linzhou people. Since she couldn't even put up with Zhinü's marriage, how could she allow the Linzhou people set foot on heaven? But with her gentle stroke, she inspired the Linzhou people to seize the gold hairpin from the god of heaven and create an artificial river.

In 1960, the Linzhou people found that the gold hairpin was right in their own hands, and they were just the Queen Mother in the myth. In order to live a fairy life, the only solution was self-reliance and hard work, through which they could turn the hammers and chisels in their hands into gold hairpins. Therefore, thousands of people worked together to split the mountains, block the Zhanghe River in the valley and divert the water to Linzhou along the cliffs, thus the water of Zhanghe River far beyond the mountains flowed into Linzhou as if from the heaven. Since then, a blue curve has appeared on the map of China, and a man-made heavenly river was born on the Taihang Mountains.

目录　　　　　　　　　　　　　　　　　　　Contents

旱魃为虐	002
Disaster of Severe Drought	003
境外引水	012
Water Diversion from outside Linxian County	013
引水之战	024
Battle for Water Diversion	025
再战总干渠	052
Another Battle of the General Main Canal	053
隔"三"修"四"	072
Constructing "the Fourth Phase" before "the Third Phase"	073

漳河水来了	082
The Water from the Zhanghe River Is Coming	083
三条干渠的修建	098
Construction of Three Main Canals	099
续建支渠配套工程	122
Continued Construction of Branch Canals	123
红旗渠带来的深刻变化	132
Profound Changes Brought about by the Hongqiqu Canal	133
附录　中国历史年代简表	148
Appendix　A Brief Chronology of Chinese History	149

旱魃为虐

水是人的命根子，而林州就是被上天卡住命根子的地方。据林州地方史志记载，从1436年到1949年的514年间，林州曾发生旱灾100多次，大旱导致的绝收30次，人相食这个令人惊心动魄的字眼出现了5次。民国初期，林县北部的桑耳庄村300多户人家，要常年到4公里外的黄崖泉担水吃。由于山高坡陡，曾跌死、跌伤多人。

1920年大旱，黄崖泉的泉水小得只有香火头那么粗。大年三十这天，桑林茂老汉起五更登上黄岸泉，想趁早挑担水回家过年。挑水的人多，一直挨到天黑他才接满一担水回村。桑家新过门的儿媳妇王水娥惦念公爹去担水一天还未回来，就出村去接。天黑路滑，新媳妇又是小脚，接过担子刚走几步，一不小心被石头绊倒，一担水洒了个净光。儿媳妇又羞又愧，就在万家团圆的除夕上吊自尽了。大年初一，桑林茂老汉埋葬了儿媳的尸体，带着全家踏上了逃荒路。从此，这一家人再无音信。可见，那时候，一担水的倾覆，足以剥夺一个人生命的尊严，足以给一个家庭带来难以承受的灾难。

除此之外，更为可怕的是人兽争水。林州马家山村5里外的西山沟，有一道从石缝里渗出的泉水，形成了一个水坑，成为人兽共用的水源地。天气越干旱，人兽争水越剧烈，不时有人因取水而葬身狼腹。

Disaster of Severe Drought

Water is the lifeblood of human beings, but Linzhou is where the lifeblood is cut off. According to the records of the local history of Linzhou, in the years from 1436 to 1949, there were more than 100 droughts in Linzhou, which caused total crop failures 30 times, with the appalling word "cannibalism" appearing five times. In the early years of the Republic of China, more than 300 households in the village of Sangerzhuang in the north of Linxian County carried drinking-water throughout the year from the Huangya Spring, which was 4 kilometers away. Due to the steep slope of the mountain, several villagers fell down the mountain, and they either died or were severely wounded.

In 1920, because of the drought, the water flowing in the Huangya Spring was so small that it was as thick as a stick of incense. On the Chinese New Year's Eve, the old man Sang Linmao set out for the Huangya Spring in the dawn and wanted to carry water home for the New Year. There were many people collecting water, and it was not until after dark that he returned to the village with two buckets of water. His newly married daughter-in-law, Wang Shui'e, was worried about the old man who hadn't come back from carrying water and she went out to meet him. It was dark and the road was slippery. The daughter-in-law was a woman with bound feet. After taking over the burden, she took only a few steps and stumbled over a stone, and two buckets of water spilled onto the ground. Wang Shui'e was so ashamed and embarrassed that she hanged herself on New Year's Eve. On the first day of the Lunar New Year, Sang Linmao buried his daughter-in-law and took the whole family on the road to flee from famine. Since then, the family has never been heard from again. It can be said that, at that time, the overturning of the two buckets of water was enough to deprive the dignity of a person's life and to bring an unbearable disaster to a family.

In addition, something worse was that humans and animals fought for water. Xishangou, which was 2.5 kilometers away from Majiashan Village in Linxian County, had a spring seeping through the cracks in the stone, which formed a puddle and became a water source shared by humans and animals. The drier the weather was, the more intense the competition was between humans and beasts. From time to time, some people were killed by wolves for drawing water. It was

据说，一个青年起五更赶早去抢水，一个十来岁的孩子中午去取水，一个妇女傍晚去担水，在不同时间，不同年龄、不同性别的三人在同一个地方，先后被狼吃了。在旧林县，为吃口水而死的人不知有多少。

干旱缺水如同一柄锋利的达摩克利斯剑，高悬在林县人民头上，高悬在这个古老县邑的生命线上。1942年大旱降临，林县饿殍遍地，惨不忍睹，老百姓在本地实在活不下去了，只好含泪告别故土，外出逃荒要饭。据不完全统计，当时全县逃荒外出的大约有10800户，占全县总户数的14%；饿死约1650人，占全县总人口的4.3‰。马鞍山村500余人，饿死约280人。采桑镇土门村王秋保一家6口饿死5口。赵老庵村41户人家，有31户背井离乡。千百年来，林县人民为逃水荒远走他乡，以致历次逃荒到外地的人数加起来比林县的常住人口还要多。

一方水土养不了一方人，这真是一种令人无可奈何的窘境。据资料统计，在1950年，全县550个村庄，需要翻山越岭远道取水的村庄就有307个。其中，到2.5公里外取水的有181个，到5公里外取水的有94个，到10公里外取水的有30个，到20公里外取水的有2个。往返十几、二十几里地挑一担水，常常要用半天时间，而这半天挑来的水仅仅够做饭和饮用，洗漱都不能保证，浇地更是无从谈起。在过去，林县每年取水多用工约在300万个以上，相当于种15万亩土地所需的劳动力。所以，林县民间流传着这样的歌谣：

家住在山间，用水真作难。

担水要翻山，吃水似油盐。

said that a young man, a ten-year-old child and a woman went to fetch water in the early morning, at noon and in the evening respectively and were eaten by wolves successively in the same place. In the old Linxian County, nobody knew exactly how many people died for water.

Drought and water shortage were like the Sword of Damocles, hanging over the heads of the people of Linxian County, hanging over the life line of this ancient county. In 1942, a severe drought made numerous people starve to death. The people could not live on in the local area, but had to bid a tearful farewell to their homeland and go out to beg for a living. According to incomplete statistics, there were about 10,800 households fleeing out of the county at the time, accounting for 14% of the total number of households in the county; around 1,650 people died of starvation, accounting for 0.43‰ of the total population of the county. More than 500 people lived in Maanshan Village and about 280 people died of starvation. Wang Qiubao, a member of Tumen Village of Caisang Town, had 6 people in his family, but 5 of them starved to death. There were 41 households in Zhaolaoan Village, and 31 families left their homes. For thousands of years, the people of Linxian County went elsewhere to escape the water shortage so that the people who fled to other places outnumbered the resident population.

The local people couldn't be nurtured by the water and land around them, which was really a helpless dilemma. According to the statistics, in 1950, among 550 villages in the county, 307 villages needed to cross mountains all the way to fetch water. Among them, 181 villages took water 2.5 kilometers away, 94 villages 5 kilometers away, 30 villages 10 kilometers away, and 2 villages 20 kilometers away. It would take half a day to fetch two buckets of water five to ten kilometers away. The water fetched in this half day was only enough for cooking and drinking, not enough for washing, let alone irrigating the fields. In the past, Linxian County needed more than 3 million man-days per year to fetch water, which was equivalent to the manpower required to plant 10,000 hectares of land. Therefore, there was such a song among the folk in Linxian County:

Living in the mountain, people cannot obtain water easily.
Crossing mountains to fetch water, they take it as oil and salt.

井口被井绳磨下的沟槽
Grooves worn by well ropes at a wellhead

在这片干旱的土地上，千百年来，这里的人们不屈不挠地与缺水的命运进行着顽强的抗争，在当时的历史条件下，千方百计地找水引水。历代主政林县的官员，文也好、武也罢，没有几个敢轻忽水务的。元朝时，潞安巡抚李汉卿路过林县，对前来迎接他的县吏说，不要为我准备什么丰盛的菜肴了，我只想好好洗个澡，以解旅途之乏。县吏面露难色，他感到十分纳闷。第二天一早，他只带了一个随从，到民间微服私访。整整一天走下来，他发现当地百姓惜水如命，一碗水反复使用过后，还舍不得倒掉。私访使他对于林县缺水的状况感触深刻。他发誓一定要解决林县老百姓的吃水问题。后来他历时3年，主持修建了一条长10公里、宽1米的天平渠，通过天平渠将天平山的山泉水引到林县县城南关的南大池，解决了沿途百姓和林县县城的吃水问题。

明弘治十七年（1504年），提学副使王勒主持修建了长10公里、宽1米、深0.7米的黄华渠。明万历二十年（1592年），滋阳举人谢思聪任

Disaster of Severe Drought

For thousands of years, the people on this arid land were tenaciously resisting the destiny of the deficiency of water. Under the historical conditions of that time, they tried every means to look for water and divert water. Among officials in charge of Linxian County of past ages, whether they were civil or military officials, few dared to neglect the water-related affairs. In the Yuan Dynasty, Li Hanqing, the governor of Lu'an, passed by Linxian County and told the official who came to meet him not to prepare any sumptuous feast for him, but to let him take a shower to relieve the fatigue of the journey. The county's official seemed embarrassed, which made Li Hanqing feel very puzzled. Early the next morning, with only one attendant, he made a private visit to the local people. After a whole day, he found that the local people cherished water as much as their lives, and after a bowl of water was used repeatedly, they were still reluctant to throw it away. The unofficial inspection trip made him deeply impressed by the deficiency of water in Linxian County. He vowed to solve the problem for the people. Later, he presided over the construction of the Tianpingqu Channel which was 10 kilometers long and 1 meter wide within 3 years. The spring water in the Tianping Mountain was led to the Nanda Pool near the south gate of Linxian County seat through the Tianpingqu Channel, which solved the problem of drinking water for the county seat and the people along the way.

In the 17th year of Hongzhi (1504) in the Ming Dynasty, Wang Le, the vice superintendent of education, presided over the construction of the Huanghuaqu Channel with a length of 10 kilometers, a width of 1 meter and a depth of 0.7 meters. In the 20th year of Wanli (1592) in the Ming Dynasty, Xie Sicong, a

林县知县。他看到林县百姓吃水艰难，想在水利上为百姓干点实事。经多方踏勘，他决定从洪谷山中引山泉水到山下的村庄。他组织十多个村庄的百姓，用了4年时间，修了一条长9公里、宽1尺的石槽渠。这条渠滋润着山下方圆几十里的土地，成了附近十几个村庄的生命渠。当地老百姓感激他引水惠民的恩德，把这条渠称作"谢公渠"，并在洪谷山中刻石立祠，供后世瞻仰。

清康熙十四年（1675年），林县人民在县城西南部引山泉水建成了桃园南渠。清乾隆十六年（1751年）林县百姓以洹河为水源，建成了南陵阳渠和武家泊渠。清末时期，漳河南岸的老百姓引漳河水分别修建了峪门口渠和古城渠，前者浇地400亩，后者灌田500亩，并种起了水稻。民国时期，林县人民以淅河水为源头修建了淅河北岸的益民渠和淅河南岸的爱民渠；以漳河为水源建设了盘阳渠。抗日战争时期，林县北部的群众以露水河为源建设了抗日渠，而林县南部的群众则引淇河水修建了荷花渠。

林县官民围绕兴水利、除旱害，书写了一部源远流长的治水史诗，治水与治县曾经并列在一起。

据统计，从元代到中华人民共和国成立之前，由于常年的干旱缺水，林县历代地方官和当地群众自发组织修建过18条大大小小、长短不

successful candidate in the imperial examinations at the provincial level of Ziyang County, became the governor of Linxian County. He found that the local people had great difficulty in drawing water and decided to do something practical for the people in water conservancy. After multiple explorations, he decided to lead the spring water from the Honggu Mountain to the village below. He organized the people of more than a dozen villages and spent four years building a stone ditch 9 kilometers long and 33 centimeters wide. This ditch nourished the land for dozens of miles below the mountain and became the ditch of life for more than a dozen villages nearby. The local people were so grateful for what he did that they named the ditch "The Ditch of Mr. Xie" after him and built a temple in the Honggu Mountain for future generations to pay tribute to him.

In the 14th year of Emperor Kangxi in the Qing Dynasty (1675), the people of Linxian County built the Taoyuan South Ditch by diverting the spring water of the mountain in the southwest of the county. In the 16th year of Emperor Qianlong in the Qing Dynasty (1751), the people of Linxian County used the Huanhe River as the source to build the Nanlingyang Ditch and the Wujiabo Ditch. In the late Qing Dynasty, the people on the south bank of the Zhanghe River built the Yumenkou Ditch and the Gucheng Ditch respectively by diverting the Zhanghe River. The former irrigated 27 hectares of land, and the latter irrigated 33 hectares of land, with rice planted. In the period of the Republic of China, the people of Linxian County built the Yimin Ditch on the north bank of the Xihe River and the Aimin Ditch on the south bank, both with the Xihe River as the source, and constructed the Panyang Ditch with the Zhanghe River as the source. During the Anti-Japanese War, people in the northern part of Linxian County built the Anti-Japanese Ditch with the Lushuihe River as the source, while the people in the southern part of Linxian County built the Lotus Ditch by diverting the Qihe River.

The officials and ordinary people of Linxian County composed an epic of water control, with the water control and the county governance equally important.

According to statistics, from the Yuan Dynasty to the founding of the People's Republic of China, because of perennial drought and water shortage, the local officials and local people in Linxian County organized spontaneously and

一的引水渠。但是，这些引水工程都只是小范围地解决了一部分老百姓的用水问题，更多的林县人民还是为缺水所困扰，况且这些引水工程一遇大的旱情大多也还会失去功效。饱受干旱缺水之苦的林县人民，祖祖辈辈因缺水而盼水，盼望天降及时雨，盼望地下有水源，盼望河中长流水，盼望山谷涌清泉，盼望吃水不出村，盼望种上水浇田。千百年来在缺水环境中苦苦挣扎的林县人想水、盼水、求水、找水，形成了一种与生俱来的恋水情结。对很多外地人来说，平淡无味的水是司空见惯、唾手可得之物。但对于林县人民来说，水是上天馈赠的珍品。你很难想象，这里会有那么多以"水"命名的村落，有那么多人的名字里带有"水""泉"等字眼。全县500多个村庄中，有300多个村子的名称与水相关，如洪河、井院、张家井、李家池、砚花水、武家水、三弓水、曹旺水、大井、水河、大河、魏家河、柳泉等，连给孩子取名也要带上水字：水生、水旺、水泉、水英、水莲、旺泉、旺水、来水、发水、生水、泉水、引水、和水、海水、明水、源水……对水的渴求，大概就是林县人民心中挥之不去的心结。

多少期盼，交给时间，多少时间，归于虚幻，当大自然赐予林县的一切资源因缺水而变得无所依赖的时候，怎样才能拯救这方干旱的土地呢？

built 18 diversion channels of different lengths and widths. However, these water diversion projects could only solve the water problem for a small proportion of ordinary people on a small scale. More people in Linxian County still suffered from water shortage. Moreover, most of these diversion projects would also lose their effectiveness in the event of major droughts. Due to the drought and shortage of water, the people of Linxian County who had suffered a lot from generation to generation dreamed of obtaining water all the time, looked forward to timely rain, looked forward to the underground water source, looked forward to water ever-flowing in the river, and looked forward to the spring water streaming out of the valleys. They expected to get water inside the village and they expected to irrigate the fields. The people of Linxian County, who struggled in a water-deficient environment for thousands of years thought of water, hoped for water, prayed for water and looked for water, and they formed an innate complex about water. For people from other places, the plain and tasteless water is commonplace and at fingertips. But for the people of Linxian County, water is a gift from heaven. It's hard to imagine that so many villages were named after "water", and so many people adopted the words "water" and "spring" in their names. Among over 500 villages in the county, more than 300 have names related to water, such as Honghe ("he" means "river"), Jingyuan ("jing" means "water well"), Lijiachi ("chi" means "pool"), Wujiashui ("shui" means "water"), Liuquan ("quan" means "spring"), and so on. Children are even given names with the word water, such as Shuisheng ("shui means "water"), Shuiwang, Shuiquan, Shuilian, etc. The thirst for water is probably a lingering knot in the hearts of the people of Linxian County.

How much time has been spent on expectations? How many expectations have been eventually turned into illusion? When all the resources that nature bestows on Linxian County became unavailable due to lack of water, how could this dry land be rescued?

境外引水

1949年10月1日，中华人民共和国成立，在领导全国各族人民完成了国家独立、人民解放的任务之后，中国共产党随之又开始为国家富强、人民幸福的这一伟大目标而奋斗。善治国者必先治水。对熟知中国历史与水利关系的执政者来说，最大限度地减少水旱灾害，保障百姓利益，始终是治国安邦的大事。在那个年代，深处太行山区的河南林县，几乎无人关注，但是水利却关乎这个古老县邑的生存与发展，兴水利、除旱魔成为治理林县的第一要务，治水与治县，在中华人民共和国成立后的林县，历史性地走到了一起。

中华人民共和国成立之初，一穷二白的面貌明明白白地写在中学历史教科书中。林县境内叫得上名的大山有7600余座，大沟约有7800道，那些无名的小沟小岭更是不计其数，近1500个大小村落分布在深山峡谷、垴尖沟边，大小山峰连环锁。林县东部丘陵地带海拔约500米，西部山地海拔近2000米。山高谷深，地势复杂。由于地处山区，交通不便，再加上缺水，贫穷就像山上的石头一样裸露在阳光下。

中国共产党领导的土地改革推动了林县农业生产力的发展，使农业经济在一个时期获得迅速发展。但是，土改后的农业经济仍然没有改变以一家一户为生产单位的小农经济性质，生产发展仍然有很大限制，许

Water Diversion from outside Linxian County

On October 1, 1949, the People's Republic of China was founded. After leading the people of all nationalities in China to complete the tasks of national independence and people's liberation, the Chinese Communist Party began to strive for the great goal of the national prosperity and people's happiness. He who governs a country well must first govern its water. For those in power who are familiar with the relationship between Chinese history and water conservancy, minimizing floods and droughts and protecting the interests of the people are always major events in governing the country and ensuring national security. In that era, there was almost no contact with Linxian County, which was deep in the Taihang Mountains, but the water conservancy was related to the survival and development of this ancient county. The development of water conservancy and elimination of drought became the first priority in the governance of Linxian County. The governing of water was closely connected with the governing of the county in Linxian County after the founding of the People's Republic of China.

At the beginning of the founding of the People's Republic of China, China was in the state of poverty and blankness, which is clearly written in the middle school history textbooks. There are more than 7,600 big mountains with names and about 7,800 ravines in the county, with countless unknown ones. Nearly 1,500 villages, large or small, are distributed in the deep mountains and valleys or at the top of the hills or by the gullies, surrounded by numerous mountains. The eastern hilly area of Linxian County is about 500 meters above sea level, and the western mountainous area is nearly 2000 meters above sea level. The terrain is complex, with high mountains and deep valleys. Because of inconvenient transportation and severe lack of water, poverty was self-evident and noticeably seen like stones on the mountains.

The land reform led by the Communist Party of China promoted the development of agricultural productivity in Linxian County and enabled the agricultural economy to develop rapidly in a period. However, the agricultural economy after the land reform didn't change the nature of the small-scale peasant economy with one household as a production unit. There were still great restrictions in the development of production development. Many farmers were

多农户无力扩大再生产,甚至连简单的再生产都无法维持。由于力量单薄,那时候要依靠农民自身进行大型的水利工程建设是不现实的,只有依靠林县党组织的强有力的组织,搞一些符合当时生产要求的力所能及的小型水利建设。在早期,林县各级党组织号召群众打旱井、挖深井,前者用于储蓄雨水,后者是挖掘利用地下水。在此基础上,进而引山泉、挖池塘。1951年冬,任村的桑耳庄村党支部动员全村群众挖了一条长3.5公里的深沟,在沟里用陶管一节一节连接起来作为管道,把黄崖泉的泉水引入村内。这条渠的建成不仅解决了全村300多户人家的吃水问题,还破天荒地发展了5亩水浇地。1955年冬季,河顺的马家山村村民决心把西沟里的泉水引进村。他们挖了一条长1.2公里的深沟,从河北彭城买来缸管一节一节对接起来埋入地下,作为输水管道,把水引进了村,解决了全村273户人家吃水难的问题,还能浇地80亩。

1956年,中国基本完成了生产资料私有制的社会主义改造,当时的农业合作化,是对中国传统生产方式和中国传统社会的一次划时代的全面改造,确立了社会主义制度,使得中国具备集中力量办大事的制度条件。1956年3月,林县县委、林县人民委员会组织民工开始修建英雄渠。该渠渠首位于山西省壶关县苏家坪,这是林县第一次尝试从外省筑坝引水。这条渠道设计干渠全长13.8公里,宽3.6米,高2米,纵坡1/1000,过水流量10立方米/秒。

unable to expand reproduction, or even sustain simple reproduction. Due to the weak strength, it was unrealistic for the peasants to carry out large-scale water conservancy projects on their own. Only by relying on the strong organization of the Chinese Communist Party, could they engage in small-scale water conservancy construction that would meet the requirements of the production at that time. In the early days, the Party organizations at all levels in Linxian County called on the people to dig dry wells and deep wells. The former was used to store rainwater, while the latter was used to utilize groundwater. On this basis, the mountain springs were diverted and the ponds were dug. In the winter of 1951, the Party branch of Sangerzhuang Village of Rencun Commune mobilized all the villagers to dig a deep ditch 3.5 kilometers long. In the ditch, earthen pipes were connected together to divert the spring water of Huangyaquan into the village. The completion of this ditch not only solved the problem of drinking water for more than 300 households in the village, but also developed 1/3 hectare of irrigated land. In the winter of 1955, the villagers of Majiashan Village of Heshun Commune decided to divert the spring water from Xigou Valley into the village. They dug a deep ditch 1.2 kilometers long, bought earthen pipes from Pengcheng of Hebei Province, and buried them into the ground as the water pipeline to transfer water to the village, which solved the problem of drinking water for 273 households in the village and also irrigated 5 hectares of land.

In 1956, China basically completed the socialist transformation of the private ownership of the means of production. At that time, the agricultural cooperation was an epoch-making comprehensive transformation of traditional Chinese production methods and traditional Chinese society. It established the socialist system and enabled China to have the institutional conditions to concentrate its efforts on major events. In March 1956, the County Committee of Linxian County and the People's Committee of Linxian County organized peasant workers to start building the Yingxiong Canal. Its headwork was located in Sujiaping, Huguan County, Shanxi Province. It was the first time that Linxian County had attempted to bring water from another province. The main canal was designed to be 13.8 kilometers long, 3.6 meters wide and 2 meters deep, with the longitudinal slope 1/1000 and a flow rate of 10 cubic meters per second.

1956年11月，任村区的盘阳、赵所、木家庄、卢家拐四个村的两千多名男女民工开始修建天桥断渠。该渠从山西平顺县马塔村附近的漳河引水，干渠长17.5公里，宽1.3米，高0.8米，纵坡1/2000，过水流量1立方米/秒。

　　1958年3月8日，林县县委召开县委扩大会议，具体研究如何全面解决林县缺水问题。经过计算，再有1亿立方米的水，即可基本解决林县全县的缺水问题，因此县委决定在淇河、淅河、露水河上分别建一座中型水库。淇河上蓄水1000万立方米的要街水库于3月24日动工，淅河上蓄水3000万立方米的弓上水库和露水河上蓄水7000万立方米的南谷洞水库于4月1日开工。

　　林县县委双脚踏在太行山上，带领全县人民找水、挖水、蓄水、引水，植树涵养水，小流域治理保水，穷尽了所能想到的一切办法，要为林县人民创造一个渠道网山头、清水到处流的新天地。到1959年，林县的水利建设成就斐然。然而，人们还没有来得及享受水利建设的成

村民们走几十里山路去担水
The villagers walking on the mountain road for dozens of miles to fetch water

In November 1956, more than 2,000 men and women peasant workers from the villages of Panyang, Zhaosuo, Mujiazhuang and Lujiaguai of Rencun Commune began to build the Tianqiaoduan Canal. The canal drew water from the Zhanghe River near Mata Village, Pingshun County, Shanxi Province. The main canal was 17.5 kilometers long, 1.3 meters wide and 0.8 meters deep, with the longitudinal slope of 1/2000 and a flow rate of 1 cubic meter per second.

On March 8, 1958, the County Committee of Linxian County held an enlarged meeting of the County Party Committee to specifically study how to comprehensively solve the problem of water shortage in Linxian County. After calculation, another 100 million cubic meters of water could basically solve the problem of water shortage in all parts of Linxian County. Therefore, the County Party Committee decided to build a medium-sized reservoir on the Qihe River, the Xihe River and the Lushuihe River respectively. The construction of the Yaojie Reservoir with a storage of 10 million cubic meters of water on the Qihe River started on March 24, and the Gongshang Reservoir with a storage of 30 million cubic meters on the Xihe River and the Nangudong Reservoir with a storage of 70 million cubic meters on the Lushuihe River came into construction on April 1.

The County Committee of Linxian County stepped on the Taihang Mountains to lead the people of the county to look for water, dig for water, store water, divert water, plant trees to conserve water and retain water in a small drainage basin. They did whatever they could to create a new world with clear water everywhere and the channel networks spreading over the mountains. By 1959, Linxian County had made great achievements in water conservancy construction. However, before people could enjoy the results of water conservancy

果，就遭遇了新的挫折。1958年一冬无雪，1959年一春无雨，林县遇到了有史以来最严重的旱灾，把全县的水利工程考了个遍。山高路远磨破了鞋，口渴只能望云彩，天上的雨积云就是地上的水，那雨水汇集流进水库、池塘、旱井就能被利用。可是这个时候老天爷却是一点面子都不给，林县人民修水库、凿旱井，但天上不降水，已建成的三大水库一点水也没有，县内2000多个池塘全干了。挖山泉、打水井地下不给水，6500多个泉眼不出水了，5700多眼水井干了4000多眼。河断流、井见底，没有了水源，已修成的渠道引水功能几乎完全丧失。

林县再也找不到可利用的水源了，干旱给全县工农业生产带来严重的损失，山区群众又开始翻山越岭远道取水了。

任何历史都是在具体的地理空间中展开的，不同的地理空间有着不同的自然条件，因自然条件不同，生活在当地的人群只能选择特定的生产、生活方式，并进而产生大不相同的对于发展的想象。千百年来，这里的人们总是千方百计把泉水引出来，把地下水挖出来，把天上的降水蓄起来。但是，这种原地引、挖、蓄的治水方式，平常年景还可以发挥效用，缓解局部地区的旱情，但一遇大旱，导致源头无水，这些水利设施也就无法发挥作用了。于是，人们又开始了新一轮的引、挖、蓄工程。这种在原地打转的治水模式，形成了一个循环往复的怪圈，圈住了林县人抗旱治水的思路。资源性的缺水，仅靠内部挖潜是解决不了根本

construction, they encountered new setbacks. There was no snow in the winter of 1958 and no rain in the spring of 1959. Linxian County encountered the worst drought in history and the county's water conservancy projects didn't stand the test of time. Because of the high mountains and far-away distance, people had their shoes worn out, and they could only gaze at the clouds when thirsty. The rain cumulus clouds in the sky would turn into water on the ground, and then the rainwater could be collected in reservoirs, ponds and dry wells and utilized. But at this time, the rain god was not helpful at all. The people of Linxian County built reservoirs and dry wells, but because it didn't rain at all, there wasn't any water in the three major reservoirs and more than 2,000 ponds were all dry. No water appeared from the mountain springs or the water wells that were newly dug. More than 6,500 springs did not produce any water, and among 5,700 water wells, more than 4,000 had become dry. The rivers stopped flowing, and the wells were empty. With no water source, the channels that had been built almost completely lost their diversion functions.

No available water sources could be found inside Linxian County. The drought had caused serious losses to the whole county's industrial and agricultural production, and the local people had to cross mountains to get water again.

History is developing in specific geographical spaces. Different geographical spaces have different natural conditions. Consequently, people living in the areas can only choose specific production modes and lifestyle, and then come up with very different ideas for development. For thousands of years, people here always made every endeavor to divert the spring water, dig up the groundwater and store rainwater. However, such water management methods as diverting, digging up and storing water in the local area could play a role in alleviating the drought in some areas, but in severe drought years, when the water sources were dried-up, these water conservancy facilities would be unable to function. As a result, people began a new round of projects to divert, dig up and store water. This kind of water management mode, which still clung to the old ideas, had formed a vicious circle, which restricted the ideas of the people of Linxian County about drought resistance and water management. It was impossible to solve the fundamental problem of resource shortage only by tapping potential from within. Water is the

问题的。水是生命之源,是人类赖以生存和发展的生命线,但向哪里要水呢?无数林县人在梦中希冀着能够早日挣脱大自然的摆布,能有一渠清亮亮的渠水流过门前。这简单而又迫切的愿望难道是一个无法圆的梦吗?

当内生资源不能满足生存需要时,引进外部资源就成为必由之路,从境外引水就成为解决林县当地缺水问题的最佳选择。林县县委把目光开始投向林县北部的浊漳河。浊漳河发源于山西省沁县,分为南、西、北三个源头。浊漳河上游主河段长约120公里,平均海拔1000米,大部分为土石山区与黄土阶梯丘陵区。各支流在中游汇合,东下至平顺县进入狭窄的峡谷地段,然后沿林县北部边界与清漳河汇合,东流入海河。在浊漳河下游两岸,除少部分黄土石地外,大部分为石山峡谷区,岩层出露,溶洞发育,悬崖高90~100米,河道宽100~200米,纵坡1/200~1/100。据当地水文资料记载,该河最大流量7000立方米/秒,一

打旱井

Digging dry wells

source of life and the lifeline for human survival and development. But where was water available? Innumerable people of Linxian County hoped that they could break free from the nature at an early date, and that there would be a clear channel of water flowing by their homes. Couldn't this wish, simple and urgent, be fulfilled?

When endogenous resources could not meet the needs of survival, the introduction of external resources became the only way, and diverting water from another province turned out to be the best choice to solve the problem of the water shortage in Linxian County. The Linxian County Committee began to turn their attention to the Zhuozhanghe River in the north of Linxian County. It originates from Qinxian County of Shanxi Province, with three sources: the southern source, the western source and the northern source. The upstream main river section is about 120 kilometers long and has an average elevation of 1,000 meters. Most of the area belongs to earth-rock mountains and loess step hilly areas. With the tributaries converged in the middle reach, the Zhuozhanghe River flows eastward to Pingshun County and enters the narrow canyon area, and then it is merged with the Qingzhanghe River along the northern boundary of Linxian County, and flows eastward into the Haihe River. Both banks of the lower reach of the Zhuozhanghe River are stone mountain canyon areas, except for a small part of loess and rocks. The rock strata are exposed and the karst caves are developed, with the cliffs 90~100 meters high, the river channel 100~200 meters wide, and the longitudinal slope 1/200~1/100. According to local hydrological data, the maximum flow of the river is 7,000 cubic meters per second, the general

般流量30立方米/秒，平均最小流量13立方米/秒，即使在中等旱年的枯水期也有8~9立方米/秒，年径流量7.3亿立方米，水量丰富，能够满足林县引水的需要。

在摸清漳河的基本情况后，林县县委决定修建红旗渠，引漳河水入林县，从而一举解决林县干旱缺水的问题。

人类社会发展的历史表明，充足的水源对于经济社会的发展有着重要的推动作用。从历史到今天，人们为了生存与发展，早已开始通过改变河流的走向以调水的手段获得必需的淡水。林县水资源短缺的客观实际,使林县的执政者在治水方略上必然要做出新的选择，最终确定以"引漳入林"的战略举措重新安排林县河山。

flow is 30 cubic meters per second, and the average minimum flow is 13 cubic meters per second. Even in the dry season of moderate drought, the flow is still 8~9 cubic meters per second. The annual runoff is 730 million cubic meters. With the abundant water, the river can meet the needs of water diversion for Linxian County.

After getting a clear picture of the Zhanghe River, the Linxian County Party Committee decided to build the Hongqiqu Canal by leading the Zhanghe River into Linxian County, thus solving the problem of drought and water shortage in Linxian County in one stroke.

The history of the development of human society indicates that adequate water sources play an important role in promoting economic and social development. From the past to the present, in order to survive and develop, people have already begun to obtain the necessary fresh water by changing the course of the rivers. The objective reality of the water resource shortage in Linxian County has made the leaders of Linxian County make a new choice in the water management strategy, and finally decide to change the current situation of Linxian County with the strategic measure of "channeling the Zhanghe River into Linxian County".

引水之战

红旗渠是1960年2月11日开工的。这一天是中国传统节日——元宵节,在中国的传统习俗中,这是一个阖家欢聚的日子。在这样的节日里,林县一群又一群的庄稼人于黎明时分,从一个个山窝里涌出来,组成浩浩荡荡的队伍,急匆匆地前行。在这支队伍中,有父子齐上阵的,有夫妻同行的,甚至还有一家三代人同去的。就是这样一群普普通通的老百姓,要劈山导河、穿山越堑,从山西省境内把漳河水引入林县,建成纵横全县1500公里的灌溉网络,把水源地与水资源贫乏之地连接起

千军万马上太行

Thousands of people were marching up the Taihang Mountains

Battle for Water Diversion

The construction of the Hongqiqu Canal started on February 11, 1960. That day was the Lantern Festival, a traditional Chinese festival for the family reunion. On a day for family gatherings, farmers in Linxian left their homes in the mountains and earnestly set out on their journey in groups. Among the large crowd of people heading for the construction site, some were fathers and sons, some were husbands and wives and some were the three generations of one single family. It was with the hard work of those ordinary people that the mountains would be tunneled, water would be diverted from the Zhanghe River of Shanxi Province to Linxian County of Henan Province and a 1,500-kilometer irrigation network would be successfully built. It was with their hard work that the land stricken with water shortage would be connected with the water abundant area and the water would be shared by people of both places. This water conservancy

来，实现水资源共享。这项水利工程沿途地质条件复杂、地势险要，堪称当时中国引水工程之最。如果没有足够的勇气，这项引水工程就只能存在于想象之中。但现在，建设者们制定了一个极具魄力的解决方案：削平1250座山头，用211个隧洞、152座渡槽实现对太行山的穿越连接。林县的第一代创业者们要用战天斗地的豪情将隔山引水的蓝图变为现实。

引漳河水入林县的渠系由总干渠、干渠、支渠、斗渠、农渠、毛渠六级渠道构成，并结合自然地质、地形条件来确定各级渠道的位置和走向。从渠首到任村公社南部边界的分水岭，就是长约70公里的总干渠，坡降的选择，取决于海拔450米的分水岭，低于这个高程灌溉范围就局限于任村公社的十几个村落。经测算，最终将总干渠的坡降确定为1/8000。要让河水"听话"，首先要在漳河干流上建一座拦水坝，把漳河水逼上右岸的太行山，使河水流入高4.3米、宽8米，设计正常流量为20立方米/秒、加大流量为25立方米/秒的人工渠道，沿浊漳河右岸绕山跨堑东行20公里进入林县境内，下行至分水岭后，再建一、二干渠分水闸，分水闸渠道底部与渠首进水闸渠道底部的高差仅10.31米。一干渠自分水闸处沿林州盆地西边太行山东侧顺等高线南下41.6公里与英雄渠汇合。二干渠沿林州盆地东北部山岭南侧顺等高线东南下行48公里，至安阳县界。三干渠在一、二干渠分水闸上游560米处的总干渠上分流，

project, built on the places with complex geology and dangerous terrains, was regarded as the most important water diversion project in China at that time. Without the heroic spirit of the local people, this water diversion project could have merely been a dream. But now the builders made a very daring plan: ready to flatten 1,250 hills, excavate 211 tunnels and build 152 aqueducts across the Taihang Mountains. The first generation of pioneers in Linxian County were determined to turn the blueprint into a reality with heroic spirit.

The canal system which diverted the Zhanghe River into Linxian County consisted of six levels of channels according to their uses: general main canal, main canals, branch canals, distribution canals, field canals and field ditches. The location and orientation of all the channels were determined by the geological and topographic conditions. The General Main Canal, with a length of about 70 kilometers, was located between the headworks of the canal and the watershed of the southern boundary of Rencun Commune. The slope of the General Main Canal was determined by the watershed with an altitude of 450 meters above sea level. Below this altitude, the scope of irrigation was only limited to a dozen of villages. After careful measures and calculations, the slope of the General Main Canal was finally determined to be 1/8000. To control the flow rate of the river, a dam had to be built first on the main stream of the Zhanghe River, and thus forced the water to flow along the Taihang Mountain on the right bank so that the water would enter the man-made canal 4.3 meters high and 8 meters wide, with the designed normal flow rate of 20 cubic meters per second and the increased flow rate 25 cubic meters per second. The canal would go east along the right bank of the Zhuozhanghe River for 20 kilometers through the hills and mountains, enter Linxian County and reach the watershed. There the diversion sluices of the First Main Canal and the Second Main Canal would be built with a height difference of a mere 10.31 meters between the bottom of the sluice channels and that of the intake of the headworks. The First Main Canal, starting from the sluice, would go south for a length of 41.6 kilometers, following the contour line, along the west of the Linzhou Basin, i.e, the eastern side of the Taihang mountain, and then join the Yingxiong Canal. The Second Main Canal would go southeast along the contour line for a length of 48 kilometers, along the southern side of the mountains in the northeast of the Linzhou Basin and enter

沿任村盆地南缘东北向盘山行走，穿过8公里隧洞后进入东岗盆地，全长12公里。各条干渠之下再分出支渠，支渠之下分出斗渠，斗渠之下再分出农渠、毛渠。为了调节用水、以丰补歉，在干、支、斗渠沿线根据灌溉所需水量，建设大小不等的库、池来储蓄丰水季节的来水。形成以引为主、引蓄结合，以灌为主、灌排结合，以自流为主、自流与提灌结合的能蓄、能灌、能排、能发电，相互调节、综合利用的灌溉网络，以满足全灌区50万亩土地灌溉和人畜用水要求。

如今，这支3.7万人的修渠队伍，瞄准的是山西省境内20公里长的总干渠第一期工程。林县最北部的任村公社的民工承担起渠首枢纽工程和1500米的渠道建设任务。

漳河水从侯壁断上猛跌下来，在峡谷中发出恐怖的咆哮声。如何才能让河水"爬"上岸边的太行山呢？这是修建红旗渠至关重要的一步。要想使河水顺利上山，必须在水中建成一道拦河坝，拦腰斩断漳河，把水位提高到需要的高度，使河水沿着预定的引水线路流进引水涵洞。

工程指挥部从2000多人中挑选的500余名骨干分子组成突击营，要向漳河开战了。但他们一无工程师，二无机器设备，使用的工具仍旧是传统的铁锤、钢钎、铁镢、铁锹、火药，再加上每个人的双手。

看着漳河水滚滚而来，他们不知从何下手。突击营营长董桃周在河两岸走了几个来回，又跟老匠人们嘀咕了半天，商定先从两岸浅水处截起，最后再集中力量截断中间的"龙口"。截流筑坝没有钢筋混凝土，

the boundary of Anyang County. The Third Main Canal, with a total length of 12 kilometers, would be diverted from the General Main Canal, 560 meters upstream of the sluices of the First Main Canal and the Second Main Canal. It would run northeast along the southern side of the Rencun Basin and then enter the Donggang Basin after going through the 8-kilometer tunnel. Under main canals, there were branch canals, and in turns there were distribution canals, field canals and field ditches. In order to adjust the use of water in different seasons, reservoirs and pools of different sizes would be built close to the canals of different levels according to the amount of water needed for irrigation, so as to store water in the rainy season, and form an irrigation network of mutual regulation and comprehensive utilization, which had the functions of storage, irrigation, drainage and power generation, with priority to water diversion and combined with storage, with priority to irrigation and combined with drainage, and with priority to artesian flow and combined with pumping, so as to satisfy the needs for water of over 33,000 hectares of land, humans and animals.

The team of 37,000 people were to construct the first phase of the 20-kilometer General Main Canal in Shanxi Province. The farmers of Rencun Commune in the northernmost part of Linxian County assumed the task of building the headworks and the 1,500-meter canal.

The Zhanghe River plunged from the Houbi cliff and roared into the valley. How could one make the river water "crawl" up the Taihang Mountains? It was a crucial step in the construction of the Hongqiqu Canal. In order to divert the water to the mountains smoothly, it was necessary to build a dam to stop the river and raise the water level to the required height so that the water would flow into the diversion culvert along the predetermined diversion line.

The Hongqiqu Canal Construction Command chose more than 500 from over 2,000 workers to form a commando team. They were to wage a war to the Zhanghe River, but they had no engineers or proper machinery but traditional tools such as hammers, steel chisels, shovels, explosives and their own hands.

Looking at the turbulent Zhanghe River, they didn't know where to start. Dong Taozhou, the commando team leader, walked a few rounds on both sides of the river observing the situation and asked some veteran craftsmen for advice. They all agreed to build the dam from the shallow areas on both banks and

只有用石头。太行山上有的是石头，但要到河两岸的高山上去开采。石头开采出来了，要从山上运到河床上又成了问题。山上原本没有路，只有民工们开采石头时踩出来的羊肠小道，盘旋十多个弯，又窄又陡。抬石头时，两人往起一站，后边高，前边低，系石头的铁绳一下子就从杠子中间滑到了前边，重量都落到了前边的人的肩上，后边的人使不上劲，前边的人站不起身。看到这种情况，营长董桃周就让人们把两人抬的石头放到他自己肩上，亲自带头背石头。就这样，民工们开始用肩膀扛料石。女民工也不示弱，跟男青年一样背石头，女青年范巧竹只一个月，鞋就穿破了4双，垫肩磨烂了6副。能背动的石头都背走了，背不动的只好一步一挪地往下滚。像蚂蚁啃骨头一样，民工们最终备齐了筑坝用的全部石料。

经过一个多月的艰苦劳动，清一色的大石坝筑在河床两侧，等待着封堵十几米宽的龙口。沙袋、草包、巨石，像小山一样堆在岸旁，人们摩拳擦掌，准备与漳河作最后的决战，成败在此一举。

20多个流量的河水，原来分布在宽阔的河床里，看起来不算太大，如今被两岸的石坝挤在十几米宽的龙口里，像一匹奔腾的野马，水流湍急。民工们向河中投下三百斤重的沙袋、草包，一触水面就被冲走了，扔下的巨石，转瞬即逝。他们又把一批批成百上千斤的大石块、大沙包一齐往下投，但还是无济于事。漳河就像永远填不饱的肚子，任你扔下多少，除了激起几朵浪花之外，不起任何作用。如果时间这样拖延下

then concentrated on closing the closure gap, the middle part of the river. There was no reinforced concrete but stones to build the dam. There were sufficient stones available on the Taihang Mountains, but the workers had to climb up the mountains to obtain them. They also had the problem to deliver stones from the mountain to the riverbed. There had been no roads in the mountains, but the narrow and steep winding trails the workers trod out when mining stones. When two workers tried to carry a stone with a pole, the worker in the front was low and the other in the back was high due to the slope, so that the wire rope that tied the stone would slip from the middle of the pole to the front. The weight would totally fall onto the shoulder of the person in the front so that he couldn't stand up, while the worker behind couldn't help at all. Seeing that, Dong Taozhou asked people to put the stone on his back and carried it to the destination. Other workers followed his example. Female workers did the same work as men did. A girl named Fan Qiaozhu wore off 4 pairs of hand-made shoes and 6 pairs of shoulder pads within a month. The workers carried all the stones that they could. Those that were too heavy to carry had to be rolled down step by step. With great effort, the workers finally collected all the stones needed for the dam.

After over a month of hard work, a big stone dam was constructed on both sides of the riverbed, leaving the closure gap over 10 meters wide to be blocked off. Sandbags, straw bags and boulders were piled on the banks like hills. People were gearing up and preparing for the last battle against the Zhanghe River. Success or failure depends on this action.

The river water over 20 cubic meters per second, originally distributed in the wide riverbed, flew slowly and peacefully. But now it was squeezed to the closure gap, a dozen of meters wide, by the stone dam on both sides of the river. The water, wild and turbulent, roared through the narrow watercourse. The workers cast sandbags and straw bags of over 150 kilograms in weight into the river, but those bags were instantly washed away and sunk into the river. Even the heavy boulders they rolled down soon disappeared into the torrents. More large stones and sandbags as heavy as hundreds of kilograms were thrown into the river, but they did not help, either. The Zhanghe River seemed to have an insatiable stomach that couldn't be satisfied forever. Whatever was cast into the river couldn't do anything except to stir up a few waves. If the time dragged on like this, there

去，等到汛期山洪暴发，截流就没有任何可能了。营长董桃周突然想到了一个办法，就是在两岸打上桩，系上几根铁丝把沙袋拦住，把龙口堵起来。大家都认为这办法可行，马上干了起来。一根根木桩打下去了，一条条铁丝在两岸上拉起来了，一袋袋沙石投下去了。千百年来狂傲不羁的浊漳河水突然要被人类所降服，它似乎被激怒了，水势更加凶猛，狠劲地向铁丝绊住的沙袋冲击着。在一遍遍的冲击中，铁丝被冲弯了，木桩也扭动起来，最后被连根拔起，伴着铁丝，瞬间消失在激流中。又一次尝试失败了，董桃周急得吃不下饭，睡不好觉。如果这"引漳入林"的第一仗失败了，会大大挫伤全体修渠民工的士气。如今，全线都在关注着这里，大伙心中都很着急。着急之际，大伙想出了一个最原始的办法：排人墙，用人挡水。

第一个跳下去的是连长张立方，第二个跳下去的是营长董桃周，激流中人们手挽手排起了人墙。河水受到阻击，发疯似的浪头一个接一个劈头盖脑地扑打过来，几乎把人墙卷走。一道人墙不行，第二道人墙又排起来了，紧接着，第三道又在水中出现了。三月的漳河峡谷，河水冰凉刺骨，用血肉之躯抵挡着冰冷凶猛河水的民工们，嘴唇冻得由红变紫、由紫变白。总指挥部送来了仅有的两瓶土产白酒，让他们喝下抵挡一下寒冷。两瓶白酒在三道人墙中传来传去，每人只有一小口。这一小口的热量刚下肚，就被寒流吸走了。人墙依然屹立着，暴躁的漳河在人墙面前一点点挣扎着，一点点退缩着。岸上的人们争分夺秒地把一根根木桩打下去，把一包包沙包、草袋投下去，把一块块料石垒起来。经过几十个小时的连续奋战，龙口终于合拢了。1960年5月1日，漳河水不得不按照人们的意志，顺利流进了红旗渠的引水涵洞。

就在任村公社的截流英雄们大战渠首拦河大坝的时候，东岗公社的

would be no possibility to stop the flow when the floods came in the rainy season. Suddenly, Dong Taozhou had an idea and suggested driving piles into both banks and tying steel wires between the piles across the river to stop the sandbags and close the river. Everyone agreed that this method was feasible and they started their work. Wooden piles were driven into both banks, steel wires were pulled up across the river, and sandbags were cast into water. The river that had been arrogant for thousands of years refused to surrender to human beings. It flew into a big fury and was getting fiercer, slamming into the sandbags that were caught by the wires. The wires were bent, and the piles were twisted and finally uprooted. Both the piles and the wires disappeared into the rapids. The attempt failed. Dong Taozhou was so eager to complete the task that he couldn't eat or sleep well. If the first phase of "channeling the Zhanghe River into Linxian County" failed, it would greatly discourage the morale of all the workers. Now the whole project paid close attention to this place and every worker present was very anxious. They came up with a most primitive method: to form human walls to block water.

Zhang Lifang, the team leader, was the first to jump into the cold water, followed by Dong Taozhou. The workers stood in the rapids, hand in hand. The river was obstructed, and the maddening waves rushed one after another, almost sweeping away the human wall. One wall of people could not stop the water, and then the second wall was formed in the water, followed by the third. The Zhanghe River was still bitterly cold in March. The workers blocked it with their flesh-and-blood bodies. Their lips were frozen from red to purple and from purple to white. The General Command sent the only two bottles of local liquor, to help the workers withstand the coldness. Two bottles of liquor were passed around among the people dipping into the cold water, each with only a sip. The heat generated by the sip of liquor was soon sucked away by the cold currents. The human walls were standing and the violent river was struggling and gradually retreating. The people on the banks were working against the clock to drive the wooden piles, cast sand bags into the river and place piles of stones. After dozens of hours of continuous work, the closure gap was finally closed. On May 1, 1960, the Zhanghe River had to follow people's will and flew into the diversion culvert of the Hongqiqu Canal.

While the heroes of Rencun Commune were building the dam across the river, Donggang commune's laborers ascended the Shizi Hill. The hill was

修渠民工登上了石子山。石子山山势险要，石质疏松，总干渠要从石子山山腰穿过。渠线下是30米高的绝壁，渠线上是150米高的鹅卵石堆积层，由于黏结度差，风一吹，乱石滚动，无法立足，当地民谣说："石子山，鬼门关，腰系白云峰触天。猴子不敢上，禽鸟不敢沾，风沙弥漫漳河岸，尘烟滚滚把路拦，吼声震得山谷响，登山还比上天难。"山体全由漳河千万年冲积的鹅卵石堆积而成，石缝之间全是流沙，缺草少树，孤独阴森。漳河河谷风大，山风从河谷冲上山顶又卷下来，鸡蛋大的石头像冰雹一样掉下来，直落漳河。在这种地方，人要上去，手无可抓之物，脚踩上去，沙石就像泥石流一样直往下涌。

按照施工设计，要在这里挖一个巨人的炮眼，炸平山头，一炮炸见渠底，打开前进的道路。民工们腰系鸡蛋粗的绳索，在山腰抡锤打钎、凿挖炮眼。人在炮眼洞里站不稳、蹲不下，上面还不时有拳头大的石头砸下来。就这样，他们轮班苦战10个昼夜，打出了一个直径3.5米、深18米的大炮眼，填装2125公斤炸药、268根雷管。一炮过后，崩倒了半架山。把几千斤炸药一次性装进一个炮眼里，充分展示了林县人民敢想敢干的创新精神。

炸崩后的石子山，沙石如雨后的山洪，整整往下倾泻了三天三夜，到第四天，仍是如此。为保证施工安全，防止乱石滚下砸伤人，民工们在倾斜角度约80°的陡坡上开挖深沟，再上山割荆棘条，编成篱笆，在渠线上方设置篱笆墙。一排篱笆一条深沟，拦住了滚石，挡住了流沙。

dangerous with loose stones, but the General Main Canal had to pass through the mountainside. Under the canal line was a 30-meter-high cliff. Above the canal line was 150-meter-high cobblestone accumulation. Due to poor adhesion, when the wind blew, the stone would roll and one couldn't stand steady. The local folk song revealed how dangerous it was, "The Shizi Hill, a gate to hell; high above the world is its peak, with clouds around its waist. Monkeys dare not to climb, birds dare not to linger. The wind blows, the sand flies, the dust dims the roads, with a roaring sound shaking the valley. It's more dangerous to climb the Shizi Hill than to ascend the heavens." The hill was formed through the accumulation of alluvial pebbles of the Zhanghe River for thousands of years. The stone cracks were filled with quicksand and one would seldom see grass or trees. It was lonely and gloomy. It was very windy in the Zhanghe River Valley. The mountain wind rushed from the valley to the top of the mountain and then rolled down. The egg-sized stones fell like the hails into the river. While climbing, one had nothing to hold on to with his hands and no steady places to put his feet on for the sands flowed like a mudslide.

According to the construction design, a huge blast hole would be dug here, and then the top of the hill would be blown up so as to open the way forward. The workers had thick ropes tied around their waists, hammering and boring at the mountainside. The blast hole was not big enough for them to stand steady or squat down. From time to time, stones as big as fists fell down. Under such circumstances, they worked in turns for 10 days and nights, and excavated a blast hole with a diameter of 3.5 meters and a depth of 18 meters, filling 2,125 kilograms of explosives and 268 detonators. After one blasting, half of the hill collapsed. Putting thousands of kilograms of explosives into one blast hole at a time fully demonstrated the daring and innovative spirit of the people of Linxian County.

After the explosion of the Shizi Hill, sand and stones fell like floods after rain for three days and nights incessantly. The situation was not improved on the fourth day. In order to ensure the safety of construction and prevent falling stones, the workers excavated deep ditches on the steep slope with an inclination of about 80°, and then cut thorns on the hill to build fences above the canal line. A row of fence and a deep ditch blocked the rolling stones and the quicksand. In order to

为了加快工程进度，民工们在山腰与河滩之间建成300多条空运线，沙筐、灰斗、料石往来穿梭，上下飞舞，施工进度逐日加快，终于征服了石子山，红旗渠继续向前延伸。

横水公社白壁连队16岁女民工栗娇美，与姐妹们用抬筐抬石渣，每次抬筐被装满后，她再捧上两捧才抬着走，每天都是超额完成任务，总是抢得先进红旗，从没落后过。连长问她敢不敢坐绳套下悬崖打炮眼，她连想都没想就说敢，于是她就坐在很粗的绳套里被放了下去。绳子是事先量好的，长度正好到施工的位置。打炮眼是三个女工一组，一人扶钎，两人抡锤。扶钎的人像壁虎一样紧贴在崖壁上，抡锤的两个人无立足之地，抡锤时用脚一蹬崖壁，往外一荡，在荡出的同时，把锤抡起来，等荡回来时把锤打在钢钎上，两个人抡锤时，一上一下，在空中荡来荡去。打不准的时候，重重的铁锤会砸在扶钎人的手上，她们也不叫痛，继续坚持。往上看，是望不到顶的高高的悬崖绝壁；往下看，是漳河滚滚的激流。从河对面望去，她们就像在峭壁间飞动的小鸟。她们就这样在悬崖绝壁上整天荡来荡去，有什么事就向上面喊话。比如钢钎掉到崖下了，喊一声，上面就给传下来一根。如果上面好久听不到打钎声，也听不到喊话声，就怀疑可能出啥事了，马上派人下来查看。她们白天打炮眼，傍晚放炮，炸出一个个小平台，以容纳更多的人下来劈山，在峭壁上开出渠道来。小小年纪的栗娇美，还不明世事，整天在悬崖绝壁上荡来荡去，她觉得就像坐在自己家的织布机上，悠然自得。队

speed up the progress of the project, the workers built more than 300 rope ways between the mountainside and the river beach. Stones and baskets carrying sand and cement mortar were delivered at a high speed. The construction progress was accelerated day by day. Finally, the Shizi Hill was conquered, and the Hongqiqu Canal continued to extend forward.

Li Jiaomei, a 16-year-old girl of Hengshui Commune, carried excavated materials with baskets with other female workers. After each basket was filled, she added two more handfuls before carrying it away. Every day she overfulfilled the task and won the red flag for advanced workers. The team leader asked if she dared to go down the cliff with safety rope and drill blast holes. She said yes without a moment's hesitation. So, she was lowered down the cliff with a very thick safety rope. The length of the rope was pre-measured and it was just long enough to reach the construction position. Three women would form one group, with one holding the steel chisel and the other two striking with the hammers. The one holding the steel chisel had to cling to the cliff like a gecko. The other two striking with the hammers had no footholds. They kicked the cliff, swung outward and raised the hammers high. While swinging back, they stroke the hammers on the steel chisel. When the two girls hammered the steel chisel, one was above the other, swinging back and forth in the air. If they missed the aim, the heavy hammers would fall on the hands of the steel chisel holder. They didn't cry in pain but continue working. Looking up, it was the cliff that extended with no end; looking down, it was the ever-flowing river. Looking from the opposite side of the river, they were like birds flying between the cliffs. They swung to and fro all day on the cliffs. When they were in need, they would call aloud to the workers above. For example, if the steel chisel fell down the cliff, they would call aloud and soon another steel chisel would be lowered from above. If no hammering sounds were sent from the cliff, those above would send people down to check if there was something wrong. They drilled holes in the daytime and made blasting in the evenings. Small platforms were excavated one after another, so that more people could come down to split the mountains and build the canal on the cliffs. At a young age, Li Jiaomei was ignorant of the world. Swinging back and forth in the air all day, she felt as if she were sitting leisurely on her own loom at home. She was reluctant to leave when the team leader wanted to send someone to replace

长要让人替换她的时候,她还舍不得。白天劳动时,她和大姐姐们叽叽喳喳说笑一天,晚上倒头便睡。晚上她一觉醒来,听到那些大姐姐们都在抱头痛哭。那个年代,山里的女孩子很少出远门,为修渠,她们远离家乡和爹娘,时间长了,会禁不住想家。一个人哭起来,其他人也跟着哭起来。

浊漳河素有"九峡十八断九十九道弯"之称,由下往上在第七道弯的南侧黄土坡上有一个村庄叫王家庄,红旗渠总干渠要从该村庄下面挖隧洞穿过。隧洞顶部就是老百姓的房屋,这里别说放炮了,震动稍微大点就会引起群众的恐慌。此外洞底都是软土,渠水一旦渗漏,不仅会造成渠道坍塌,还有可能引起滑坡,这是当地群众最担心的事情。原来距王家庄10多公里的漳河边,有个车当村,也坐落在黄土坡上。1953年汛期连降暴雨,洪水泡软了地基,引起滑坡,几十座院落全部滑入漳河,造成巨大的财产损失和人员伤亡。王家庄与车当村的地质条件相同,因此群众的担心并不多余。可不可以让渠道改线绕过村庄呢?但是,往里绕是高耸的太行石壁,往外绕则是深深的漳河峡谷,改线绕村的方案显然不可行。况且渠线的落差是固定的,抬高或降低都行不通。工程指挥部的领导和技术人员在向当地群众调查走访的基础上,对该处的地质、地形情况进行了反复勘探和测量,最终决定修改施工方案。将原设计的单孔洞改为双孔洞,以此缩小隧洞的跨度和断面,增加承受力,确保洞顶居住者的永久安全。此外,在隧洞内采取高标准衬砌措施防渗,用混凝土铺设渠底,用料石砌渠墙券洞顶,防止渠水渗漏而引发滑坡。在村

her. During the daytime, she talked happily with those older girls while working and fell asleep fast at night. Once, she woke up and heard the older girls crying. At that time, the girls in the mountainous areas rarely left their homes. In order to build the canal, they were far away from their hometowns and their parents. They missed their families deeply. Once a girl cried, the others would soon be affected and started to cry.

The Zhuozhanghe River was known for "nine gorges, eighteen sections and ninety-nine turns". A village called Wangjiazhuang was sitting on a loess slope on the south side of the seventh turn. A tunnel would be dug under the village as part of the Hongqiqu General Main Canal project. The farmers' houses were on the top of the tunnel. The slight vibration would shake the houses and cause panic among the villagers, not to mention the blasting. In addition, the bottom of the tunnel was soft earth. Once the canal water leaked, it would not only cause collapse of the canal, but also a landslide. This was what the villagers were worrying about the most. There used to be a village called Chedangcun, 10 kilometers away from Wangjiazhuang. It was also located on a loess slope. In 1953, it rained heavily during the flood season. The floods softened the foundation and caused the landslides. Dozens of courtyards slipped into the Zhanghe River, causing huge property losses and severe casualties. The geological conditions of Wangjiazhuang and Chedangcun were the same, so the local people's worries were justifiable. Could the canal line be changed so as to be away from the village? However, the village was situated between the towering stony walls of the Taihang Mountains and the deep valley of the Zhanghe River. It was obviously not feasible to change the route. Moreover, the drop of the canal line was fixed, and raising or lowering would not work. After conducting repeated explorations and measurements of the geological and topographical conditions of the site on the basis of investigation and visits to the local people, the leaders and technicians of the Construction Command finally decided to modify the construction plan. The single-hole tunnel in the original design was changed to a double-hole tunnel so as to reduce the span and section of the tunnel, increasing the bearing capacity and ensuring the permanent safety of the inhabitants. In addition, high-standard lining measures were adopted to prevent seepage in the tunnel. The bottom of the tunnel was paved with concrete, and the walls and top of the tunnel were lined with masonry

外渠道上游增建一座控制水闸，用于调节水量。修改后的设计方案，满足了当地群众的要求。施工开始后，指挥部严令施工人员，在遇到硬石层时只准放小炮不准放大炮。为加快工程进度，民工们又打了四个竖井，增加了工作面，可是外运掏出来的土石方却成了问题，民工们外运一筐土要在村里拐无数个弯，走300多米，费时耗力还影响挖洞进度。然而，再大的困难也难不倒英雄的林县人民，他们设计出了转盘轨道，打造出木制罐车，8个出渣口共铺设8条总长3100米的轨道，罐车在轨道上飞跑，与原来的人抬肩挑相比，工作效率大大提高。历时4个月后，施工队终于打通了这座长243米、每孔跨径2.5米的穿村隧洞，王家庄群众把它命名为"安全隧洞"。

泽下公社把1923米的修渠任务分为4个作业段，其中最艰险的300多米长的一段分配给了由马兰、碾上、沟窑头三个村民工编成的民工营，营长是马兰村大队长王磨妞。接到任务后，王磨妞带着碾上、沟窑头两个连的技术员到现场安排任务。这里从漳河河床到崖顶有600米高，渠线从悬崖腰部穿过。在直上直下的崖壁间，向外凸出来一大块巨石，足有百十米宽，像伸出的老虎嘴。而渠线恰恰要从这里穿过，只有先敲掉这张"老虎嘴"才能开凿渠道。从上往下看，让人头晕目眩；从下往上看，"老虎嘴"龇牙咧嘴，阴森可怕。作为营长，王磨妞自己先把最难干的一段揽下，其他两个连队在"老虎嘴"一左一右展开施工。

第二天马兰连的民工来到了"老虎嘴"的崖顶上，往下一看，个个都本能地往后缩："这要掉下去就摔成肉酱啦！"王磨妞看到大家有

to prevent leakage and landslide. A control sluice was added upstream of the canal outside the village to regulate the amount of water. The revised design met the requirements of the local people. After the construction began, the Construction Command strictly ordered the construction personnel to make small blasting only and forbid big blasting when encountering the hard rock layers. In order to speed up the progress of the project, the workers excavated four more shafts to increase the working faces. However, mucking became a problem. The workers had to make countless bends in the village and walk more than 300 meters. It was a time-consuming and labor-intensive work and would affect the progress of tunneling. However, the more difficult the tasks, the braver the people of Linxian County. They designed turntable rails and invented wooden wagons. Eight pairs of rails, with a total length of 3,100 meters, were built for eight mucking tunnels. The wooden wagons ran on the rails. Compared with transportation on shoulders, the work efficiency was greatly improved. After 4 months' work, the construction team finally completed the 243-meter-long tunnel with a diameter of 2.5 meters per hole. The villagers of Wangjiazhuang named it "Safe Tunnel".

Zexia Commune divided the 1923-meter-long canal line into four working sections. The most difficult section, more than 300 meters long, was assigned to the construction team composed of workers from three villages: Malan, Nianshang and Gouyaotou. Wang Moniu, the production brigade leader of Malan Village, was appointed as the team leader. After receiving the task, Wang Moniu took the technicians of the three villages to the construction site. It was 600 meters high from the riverbed to the cliff top, and the canal line would pass through the waist of the cliff. Between the straight cliffs, a large boulder protruded outwards, which was a hundred meters wide, like a protruding tiger mouth. The canal line just needed to pass through the "tiger mouth". Only by knocking down this "tiger mouth" could the canal be built. Looking down from the top, people felt dizzy; Looking up from the bottom, the "tiger mouth" seemed frightening. As the team leader, Wang Moniu chose the most difficult task, and the other two villages undertook the construction on the left and right sides of the "tiger mouth".

On the second day, when the laborers of Malan Village came to the top of the cliff on the "tiger mouth" and looked down, all of them instinctively shrank back. "One would turn into meat sauce once he falls off!" Sensing fear in the workers'

畏惧情绪，就说道："'老虎嘴'是死的，人是活的，活人还治不了死老虎？！"说着他就往腰间系绳子，要第一个下崖。他侄子王元锁拦住他，说要下应该自己先下。王磨妞对王元锁说："你不能下，你还没成家，我有孩子了，死了也有后代了。"王元锁说："你说的不对，你有家就应该想到他们，我没成家，一个人干净，死了也没啥后顾之忧。"

大战"老虎嘴"
A fierce battle in the Tiger Mouth Cliff

mind, Wang Moniu said, "The 'tiger mouth' is dead, and we are alive. Couldn't we defeat the dead tiger?!" While speaking, he tied a rope around his waist and was ready to go down the cliff. Wang Yuansuo, his nephew, stopped him and said that he should go down first. Wang Moniu said to Wang Yuansuo, "You can't go down. You haven't gotten a family yet. I have had children. Even if I died, I have already had descendants." Wang Yuansuo said, "No. Since you have a family, you should think of them first. I am not married and I have no worries if I died." Neither

两个人各不相让,争来争去最后两人都下去了。关键时刻第一个下,用生命做出无悔的选择;危险关头,带"长"的人先上,党员先上,结了婚的先上,弟兄多的先上。第一个人上去了,就有第二个、第三个……

在王磨妞的带领下,30多个精壮的中青年先后下到了"老虎嘴"上。他们腰系绳索,手抡大锤,在崖壁上打炮眼。山上的石英砂岩无比坚硬,钢钎打断了一根又一根,炮眼却打不下去。王磨妞与技术员宋景山以及王元锁三人从"老虎鼻子"爬上去,寻找相对较好打炮眼的位置。经过多方查看,他们找到了一条横向的破碎岩层带,决定就从这里下手打炮眼。

他们把铺盖搬来,吃住都在工地上,经过半个月的敲打,打出了7个直径2米、深12米的炮眼。全连民工用了4天时间,将500公斤炸药装进了炮眼中。最终,一次性把"老虎嘴"彻底炸掉了。接着他们又先后放了10多炮,炸开了一条宽8米、高9米的通道用于砌渠。

放过炮后的岩壁,不时会有松动的石块落下,非常危险,不除掉这些险石,就不能下崖垒砌渠道。王磨妞抓起绳索就往身上套,要下崖去除险石。王元锁、宋景山不让他下崖,要下他们下。王磨妞说:"你们都不能下,因为咱们没经验,一不小心就要了命。我是党员,又是营长,我不下心里没底,你们别争了。"三人各不相让,最后还是一起下去了。当王磨妞下到70米处时,一块石头砸在他的后背上,他抬头往上看时,又有几粒碎石砸在脸上,两颗大牙被砸掉,脸也被砸破出血了。他顾不上伤痛,挥动撬杠,把一处处松动的石块撬下,撬下的石块哗啦啦地滚进漳河,激起阵阵水花。

鸻鹆崖峭壁直立,红旗渠要从这里穿过,这就需要在鸻鹆崖上打出39个20多米深的大炮眼,分四层下切,把长近200米、高出地面近250米

man would give in, and finally they both went down. At the dangerous moments, the leaders, the Party members, the married and those with more brothers would march on. The first person came, and then the second and the third and more followed.

Under the leadership of Wang Moniu, more than 30 young and middle-aged workers successively reached the "tiger mouth". They tied ropes around their waists, held hammers in their powerful hands, and drilled blast holes on the cliff. The quartz sandstone on the mountain was extremely hard, and the steel chisels broke one after another, but the blast holes couldn't be made. Wang Moniu, Wang Yuansuo and Song Jingshan, a technician, climbed up from the "tiger nose" to find a relatively good position for blast holes. After many inspections, they found a horizontal broken rock belt and decided to excavate blast holes there.

They ate and slept on the construction site. After half a month of hard work, they excavated seven blast holes with a diameter of 2 meters and a depth of 12 meters. It took four days for the laborers to install 500 kilograms of explosives into the blast hole. In the end, the "tiger mouth" was completely blown up all at once. Then they blasted more than 10 times and blasted a channel 8 meters wide and 9 meters high for the construction of the canal.

After blasting, loose stones fell from time to time. If loose stones were not removed, it was not possible to build the canal under the cliffs. Wang Moniu tied the rope around his waist, ready to remove the stones from the cliff. But he was stopped by Wang Yuansuo and Song Jingshan. They thought they were the right persons to go down to remove the loose stones. Wang Moniu disagreed. He said that it was too dangerous, he was a Party member and the team leader, and he should go down first. None of the three men would give in, and finally they went down together. When Wang Moniu went down to 70 meters, a stone slammed on his back. When he looked up, a few small stones fell on his face. Two teeth were knocked off and his face was wounded. He had no time to care for himself, but waved the crowbar and pried up loose rocks one after another. The rocks fell into the Zhanghe river, causing a burst of waves.

The Hengwu Cliff, nearly 200 meters long and 250 meters high above the ground, was upright and steep. Since the Hongqiqu Canal would go through the cliff, it was required to drill 39 blast holes, over 20 meters deep each, and lower

的鸻鹉崖从上向下直劈80米，劈出建大渠所需的平面来，才能砌渠墙，让渠水通过。在上无寸物可攀、下无立足之地的悬崖峭壁上，修渠民工腰系绳索，抡锤打钎，凌空施工。经过连续爆破之后，山石松动，摇摇欲坠，危险随时都会发生。1960年6月12日，鸻鹉崖发生一次重大伤亡事故。这天，悬崖上一块巨石突然坍塌，滚石冲进施工人群当中，碾出一条血路滚下山去，当场造成9死3伤。这也是修渠大军进驻鸻鹉崖之后发生的第三次施工事故。一连串的伤亡事故之后，一种异常阴郁的气氛

凌空除险
Removing dangerous stones from the steep cliff

the cliff by 80 meters in four layers to form a platform, where the canal was to be constructed. On the steep cliff where there were no footholds, the workers waved hammers to drill blast holes in the air, with ropes tied around their waists. After continuous blasting, the rocks were loosened, on the verge of collapse, and dangers could happen anytime. On June 12, 1960, a major casualty accident occurred on the Hengwu Cliff. That day, a huge rock suddenly collapsed and rushed into the crowd on the construction site, leaving 9 dead and 3 injured. It was the third accident that occurred after the workers started their work on the Hengwu Cliff. After a series of casualties, an unusually gloomy atmosphere enveloped the construction site. If the construction was to be continued, the way

笼罩在施工工地上。如果要继续施工，必须想办法除掉山崖上松动的危石。然而，一块块巨石悬在直上直下的峭壁上，除非长了翅膀，普通人又如何上得去呢？在修建红旗渠的人群当中，一支专门负责除险的队伍组成了，共产党员任羊成担任除险队长。除险队员们把绳子的一端固定在悬崖顶部，然后用钢钎组成坚固的三角套桩，绳子经由套桩缓冲后，另一端牢牢系在除险人的腰间。每三名队员为一个除险小组，一人下崖除险，另外两人时刻在峰顶看护绳子，控制绳子的下放长度及确保安全。对除险人员来说，这项工作没有任何经验可以借鉴，除险者不但需要具备熟练的攀登技术，更需要过人的勇气和胆量。

在鸻鹉崖东段，有一片凹进去的石壁，叫鸻鹉檐，除险者只能像荡秋千一样，借助绳子摆动的惯性接近石壁，在与石壁接触的瞬间，精准而有力地除掉险石。山谷内山风呼啸，除险者就像随风飞舞的风筝，在半空中团团旋转，绳子随时都有可能被锋利的山石绞断，除险人随时可能跌入万丈深渊。而且，一旦身体在空中失去控制，身体与崖壁相撞，就会粉身碎骨。即使这两方面都不出意外，除险者头顶上方的碎石也时

任羊成
Ren Yangcheng

to get rid of the loose stones on the cliff had to be found. However, large rocks hanging on the vertical cliff, how could people go up? Among the workers, a team was set up responsible for the removal of dangerous rocks, with Ren Yangcheng as the team leader. The team members fixed one end of the safety rope to the top of the cliff, and installed a firm triangular pile with steel chisels. Buffered by the triangular pile, the other end of the rope was firmly attached to the waist of the stone-remover. Every three workers formed a stone-removal team, with one going down to remove the stones and the other two taking care of the rope at the top, controlling the length of the rope and ensuring the safety of the stone-remover. The stone-remover had no experience to learn from. He not only had to be skillful in climbing, but also needed extraordinary courage.

In the eastern part of the Hengwu Cliff, there was a concave stone wall called the Hengwu Eave. The stone-remover could only approach the stone wall with the help of the inertia of the swinging rope and remove the dangerous stones precisely and forcefully at the moment of his contact with the stone wall. The mountain winds roared in the valley, and the stone-remover was like a kite flying with the wind, turning in the midair. The rope could be very likely cut off by the sharp stones, and the stone-remover might fall into the abyss at any time. Moreover, once he lost control in the air, he might collide with the cliff wall and be broken into pieces. Even if the aforementioned things didn't happen, the gravels above the stone-remover's head were always threatening his life. It was

刻在威胁着他们的生命安全。难怪当时有句口头禅："除险队长任羊成，阎王殿里报了名。"要说林县人凭勇气修渠，不如说林县人在用生命修渠。几乎每一个修渠的人都曾经遇到过各种各样的危险。没办法，在当时，要活命，只有修渠，而要修渠，当时也只有这样的条件。在困难的现实面前，他们别无选择。1960年9月，红旗渠渠道顺利通过鸻鹉崖。

1960年10月1日，红旗渠总干渠山西省境内工程竣工通水，红旗渠水流进了林县边境。这是人类第一次从太行山的悬崖陡壁上开凿出一条宽8米、高4.3米、过水流量25立方米/秒的人工河流。修建这条20公里长的人工河流，斩断了45道山崖，搬掉了13座山头，填平了58道沟壑，闯过了狼脸崖、老虎嘴、太岁峰、红石崭、石子山、风沙崭、鸻鹉崖等天险，钻透7个山洞，建成大小水工建筑物45座，共完成土石砌方488万余立方米。漳河水破天荒地流到林县边境，远水可以解近渴，人们心中不再有所怀疑。人们已经看到了希望，但是前面距总干渠尽头所在地分水岭还有漫长的50公里。

那是一个饥渴的年代。1960年春，中国遇上了严重的自然灾害，自此开始，全国性的自然灾害持续三年，粮食歉收、物资短缺成为经济发展的拦路虎，我国开始进入三年困难时期。在这样一个时代大背景下，红旗渠总干渠工程只得暂时下马，等待着国家经济形势的好转。

no wonder that there was a mantra at the time, "Ren Yangcheng, the team leader, registered in the nether world." The People of Linxian County built the canal not so much with their courage as with their lives. Almost every person who built the canal encountered various kinds of dangers. They had no choice but to build the canal because water diversion was a matter of life or death for them. To build the canal, they had nothing to resort to besides what they had at hand. In the face of difficult realities, they had no choice. In September 1960, the Hongqiqu Canal passed through the Hengwu Cliff smoothly.

On October 1, 1960, the part of the Hongqiqu General Main Canal in Shanxi Province was completed and the water flowed into Linxian County. It was the first time that humans had excavated a man-made river with a width of 8 meters, a height of 4.3 meters and a flow rate of 25 cubic meters per second on the steep cliffs of the Taihang Mountains. For the construction of the 20-kilometer-long man-made river, the People of Linxian County cut off 45 cliffs, flattened 13 hills, filled 58 gullies, conquered the Wolf Face Cliff, the Tiger Mouth, the Taisui Peak, the Hongshizhan Cliff, the Shizi Hill, the Fengshazhan Cliff, the Hengwu Cliff and so on, excavated 7 tunnels and built 45 various hydraulic structures, with a total of 4.88 million cubic meters of excavation and masonry completed. For the first time, the Zhanghe River flowed to the border of Linxian County, and the water from the distant place could satisfy the need of the People of Linxian County. People no longer had doubts. Hope grew in their minds, but there was another 50 kilometers to the watershed, which was the end of the General Main Canal.

It was a time of hunger and thirst. In the spring of 1960, China suffered from a serious natural disaster, and it lasted for three years. The crop failure and the shortage of materials became the roadblocks for the economic development. China entered a difficult three-year period. Under such an era, the construction of the Hongqiqu General Main Canal had to be temporarily suspended, waiting for the economic recovery of the nation.

再战总干渠

1961年6月17日,红旗渠总干渠工程复工,开始投入第二期工程建设。由于还处于经济困难时期,第二期工程10公里的渠道就由13个公社的6000余民工修建。

青年洞是红旗渠总干渠的咽喉工程,早在红旗渠总干渠全线开工之时,就由横水公社民工负责施工。1960年3月6日,林县县委决定缩短战线,集中所有民工先建成山西省境内的第一期工程,但作为第二期工程范围内的青年洞工程,施工的民工则没有跟着转移,而是留下来继续开凿。1960年11月,整个中国遭遇到了全局性的自然灾害,中央下达关于

红旗渠总干渠
The Hongqiqu General Main Canal

Another Battle of the General Main Canal

On June 17, 1961, the construction of the Hongqiqu General Main Canal was resumed and the second phase of construction began. In such a difficult period, the 10-kilometer-long canal of the second phase was built by more than 6,000 peasant workers from 13 communes.

The Youth Tunnel was the key project of the Hongqiqu General Main Canal. As soon as the construction of the Hongqiqu General Main Canal started, the construction of the Youth Tunnel was carried out by the workers of Hengshui Commune. On March 6, 1960, the Linxian County Party Committee decided to shorten the construction line and concentrate all the workers on the construction of the first phase of the project in Shanxi Province. However, the construction of the Youth Tunnel did not stop although it was within the scope of the second phase of the project. The workers continued the excavation. Since the whole of China encountered a natural disaster, the central government issued a document on the "100 days of suspending" in the difficult period in November 1960. All the

困难时期"百日休整"的文件,所有在建的大型工程要全部停工,等待国家经济形势好转。在红旗渠总干渠全线工程下马停工的同时,县委留下300名青壮民工,承担起凿通青年洞的任务,他们苦战一冬一春,终于迎来了第二期工程的开工。

　　隧洞的洞口就开在巍峨耸立的人称"小鬼脸"的山崖上。山的外侧弓形的崖壁直上直下,高耸险峻。山那边是一条叫寺沟的深涧。渠线被山所阻挡,是绕山开渠还是顺山凿洞,必须经过科学论证。绕山开渠施工简单,工作面大,可以集中优势兵力打歼灭战,但会遇到悬崖峭壁和风化塌方;顺山凿洞则渠线短,工程量小,将来通水后水量损失也小,但开隧洞工作面小,工序繁多,工期较长。这种山势陡峭、渠线较长并且表层岩石不够完整的地形、地质状况,若绕山修明渠,大批人员要从山顶上用绳索吊下来,悬空操作,难度大,工效低,石质较差的表面岩石随时都会引发大面积塌方,施工危险性极高。一般来讲,在同一岩石地质条件下,若绕山修明渠长度超过开凿隧洞长3倍时,采用隧洞方案就比较有利。隧洞又分为横山洞和顺山洞。横山洞为从山中直穿过去,顺山洞则随着山势走向该曲则曲、该弯则弯。最终设计者确定的设计方案是在青年洞上段的400米顺山开洞,下段的200米横山穿洞。虽然洞内均为坚硬的石英砂岩,石质坚硬,但岩石完整,不易塌方,比较安全。

large-scale projects under construction should be suspended until the national economy was improved. While the entire project of the Hongqiqu General Main Canal was suspended, the County Committee left 300 young and strong workers to undertake the task of excavating the Youth Tunnel. They worked hard for a winter and a spring, and finally the second phase of the project started.

The tunnel entrance was on a towering cliff, which was called "little ghost's face". The arched cliffs on the outside of the mountain were straight, towering and precipitous. On the other side of the mountain was a deep ravine called Sigou. In view of the fact that the canal line was blocked by the mountain, it must be scientifically demonstrated whether to build a canal around the mountain or dig a tunnel through the mountain. The former was simple to construct. Due to the large working face, a large number of workers could be gathered to complete the construction quickly, but there would be troubles, such as steep cliffs and weathering landslides. The latter had the advantages of short channel lines and small quantities of work. In the future, after the water was supplied, the loss of water was also small. However, the working face of tunneling was small, with many procedures and a long construction period. In this kind of terrain and geological condition with steep mountain, long canal line and incomplete surface rocks, if a canal was built around the mountain, a large number of workers had to be suspended from the top of the mountain with ropes, which was difficult and low in work efficiency. The surface rocks with poor stone quality would cause large-area landslides at any time, thus causing extremely high construction risks. Generally speaking, under the same geological conditions, if the length of the open channel around the mountain was 3 times longer than that of the excavated tunnel, it was more advantageous to adopt the tunnel scheme. There were two types of tunnels: the Hengshan Tunnel and the Shunshan Tunnel. The Hengshan Tunnel passed straight through the mountain, and the Shunshan Tunnel was built in a zigzag way according to the terrain of the mountain. The final design plan determined by the designer was to build a 400-meter Shunshan tunnel in the upstream section of the Youth Tunnel and a 200-meter Hengshan tunnel in the downstream section. Although the hard quartz sandstone in the tunnel made construction difficult, it was relatively safe because the rock was complete and not prone to collapse. In addition, it was also possible to build adits to facilitate

此外，还可以开旁洞，有利于通风、出渣、增加工作面。同时渠线长度也会大大缩短，工程开挖量少，可以节省人力物力投入。

隧洞方案确定后，就是选择洞线。洞线的选择是否合理直接关系到工程数量、施工难易、施工安全和工程质量等一系列问题。在正常情况下，确定洞线之前，先要进行地质勘探，了解隧洞地质情况后，再进行方案比较，最后确定洞线位置。但是在对青年洞选线时，既没有钻探设备，又没有地质资料。当地群众祖祖辈辈生活在这里，长期与穷山恶水作斗争，生活就是同岩石打交道，积累了丰富经验。虽然他们说不出地质学上的专有名词，但对岩石的性状、断层的走向、节理的发育等情况，都有一定的了解。工程设计人员紧紧依靠当地群众进行了现场勘查，与当地群众紧密结合，摸清了该工程段岩石的性状、节理发育情况，比较好地确定了隧洞的洞线。

"顺山开洞顺山走，防止洞壁被穿透。"顺山开洞对洞壁厚度的控制，既不能太厚，也不能太薄，要根据地质情况作适当选择。顺山开洞都要另开旁洞，以增加工作面和便于出渣。洞壁过厚，旁洞开挖方量增大；洞壁偏薄，爆破时容易损坏洞壁，甚至把洞壁穿透。当山体岩石坚硬完整时，控制厚度为4到5米；若山壁石质较差，其厚度可适当增加。卢家拐隧洞外侧山壁石质不够完整，控制厚度为6到8米。要减少开挖量，就要缩小隧洞断面，相应地就要加大坡降。青年洞高5米、宽6.2

ventilation and mucking, and increase the working faces. At the same time, the length of the canal line would be greatly shortened and the amount of excavation would be less, which could save manpower and material resources.

After the tunnel plan was determined, the tunnel line had to be selected. Whether the selection of tunnel line was reasonable or not was directly related to a series of problems, such as engineering quantity, construction difficulty, construction safety and engineering quality. Under normal circumstances, geological exploration should be carried out before determining the tunnel line. After finding out the geological conditions of the tunnel, scheme comparison should be carried out, and finally the location of the tunnel line should be determined. However, there was neither drilling equipment nor geological data when selecting the tunnel line. The local people had lived here for generations and struggled with the harsh natural conditions for a long time. They had accumulated rich experience through their life closely related to rocks. Although they didn't know the proper terminology of geology, they had a certain understanding of the properties of rocks, the direction of faults, and the development of joints. With the help of the local people, the engineering designers conducted on-site investigation and found out the characteristics of the rock and joint development of the project section, thus determining the tunnel line.

"The tunnel should be excavated according to the topography of the mountain to prevent the tunnel wall from being cut through." If the tunnel was excavated along the topography of the mountain, the thickness of the tunnel wall should be determined according to the geological conditions, neither too thick nor too thin. And in this case, it was necessary to dig adits to increase working faces and facilitate the transportation of excavated material. If the tunnel wall was too thick, the amount of excavation in the adit would increase; if the wall was too thin, it was easily destroyed or even penetrated during blasting. When the rock of the mountain was hard and complete, the thickness of the tunnel wall should be between 4 and 5 meters; if the rock quality was poor, the thickness could be increased appropriately. The rock on the outer side of the Lujiaguai Tunnel was not complete and the thickness of the tunnel wall should be between 6 and 8 meters. To reduce the amount of excavation, it was necessary to reduce the tunnel section and correspondingly increase the tunnel gradient. The Youth Tunnel was

米，因此坡降为较陡的1/1500，减少了过水断面，节省了对坚硬岩石的开挖量。卢家拐隧洞顺山开凿，随山势弯曲，既是渠线通行的需要，也预示着未来施工的曲折进程。

1960年2月15日，横水公社卸甲坪连的王来金和九家庄连队的青年民工贾九虎腰系绳索，从山顶上下来凌空作业，在崖崭上挖出炮眼，打响了隧洞开工的第一炮，先炸出走向"小鬼脸"工作面的通道。四名炮手从下方用高木杆把炸药包顶在崖壁上放炮，上下齐运作，硬是在峭壁上炸开了一条梯形小道，为施工扫清了外围障碍，然后才是大部队上阵。缥缈的云雾，遮掩着漳河峡谷的幽深，突兀的巨崖昂然伫立在苍穹之下，带着久远岁月的印痕，铮铮地透着幽光。"小鬼脸"就像一块完整的巨岩，石英砂岩的硬度高于一般的铁制工具，一锤打下去，钢钎只能留下一个小白点，一天的进度只有30厘米。按照这样的施工进度，就算两头同时施工开挖，别说整个总干渠，仅616米的青年洞就至少需要5年的时间。这个方案绝对行不通，必须采取新的措施。经过计算，新的施工方案产生了，在隧洞外侧的绝壁上多打开5个旁洞，把616米长的隧洞分为6段，每段的路线都接近直线，原来因为隧洞的弯曲造成的施工难度降低了，而每个旁洞都可以双向施工，同一时刻就有12个工作面同时施工，既增加了工作面，又方便通风、出渣，实行长隧短打、分兵包抄的战法能够提高工作效率。

5 meters high and 6.2 meters wide, with a rather steep gradient of 1/1500, thus reducing the cross section of water and saving the amount of hard rock excavation. The Lujiaguai Tunnel was excavated along the mountain and bent with the terrain, which was not only necessary for the canal to pass through the mountain, but also an indication of the tortuous process of future construction.

On February 15, 1960, Wang Laijin and Jia Jiuhu, two farmers from the Xiejiaping Team and the Jiujiazhuang Team of Hengshui Commune respectively, tied ropes around their waists, came down from the top of the mountain to drill blast holes in the cliff. This was actually the beginning of the tunnel construction. It was planned to excavate a passage to the "little ghost's face" working face. Four blasters supported satchel charges on the cliff from below with high wooden poles, cooperated with other workers and blasted a trapezoidal path on the cliff. Only after clearing the obstacles for the construction, could the construction team enter the construction site. Misty clouds covered the deep valley of the Zhanghe River, and protruding giant cliffs stood towering under the sky, reflecting dim light with the imprints of long years. The "little ghost's face" was like a complete giant rock, and the hardness of its quartz sandstone was higher than that of ordinary iron tools. Every time the workers hit the steel chisel with a hammer, there was only a small white spot left on the rock. In this way, the daily progress was only 30 centimeters. According to this construction progress, even if the tunnel was excavated from both ends at the same time, the Youth Tunnel with a length of 616 meters would take at least five years to complete, not to mention the whole General Main Canal. This plan would definitely not work. New measures must be taken. After calculation, a new construction plan was created, i.e., five adits were dug in the cliff outside the tunnel, and the 616-meter-long tunnel was divided into six sections. In this way, the route of each tunnel section was close to a straight line. The construction difficulty caused by the curved route of the tunnel was reduced. In each adit, the excavation of the main tunnel could be carried out in two directions. Thus, the excavation could be carried out in 12 working faces simultaneously. Not only the working faces were increased, but also the ventilation and the mucking were facilitated. The strategy of dividing the long tunnel into several short ones and grouping the workers to work in different tunnel sections could improve the work efficiency.

需要开凿的5个旁洞,有3个都位于高崖之腰,而这里的高崖却是上下两端外凸中间凹陷,人称"锅腰崖"。民工们就在崖顶上打下两根钢钎,每根钢钎上系一条鸡蛋粗的麻绳,两个炮手顺着绳索下到洞线标高的地方打炮眼,炸开洞口。负责打2号旁洞的第二突击队,队长是郭家窑大队队长郭福贵。他带着两个炮手,腰系绳索从山顶下崖,往下看几十丈深的沟谷令人目眩,往上看巨石压顶让人喘不过气来。他们时而像树叶一样在空中飘荡,时而像壁虎一样紧贴崖壁。第二突击队在郭福贵的带领下,以精卫填海的精神,一锤锤、一钎钎地与岩石硬碰硬,一寸一寸地向大山腹地掘进。每天收工后,他组织大家总结当天的施工经验,找出存在的问题,鼓励大家多动脑筋、多想办法,提高工效。他曾6次负伤,每次负伤后都是强忍着疼痛,不告诉别人,想方设法瞒着上级领导,目的是不离开工地。他的背部被砸伤了,上级领导发现他的背部有血迹,就问他怎么回事。他回答说,生了个疮,不碍事。一天晚上,隧洞里刚放过炮,他第一个进洞去除险石。他一手提着马灯,一手抡锤,敲去放炮后震松的险石。正在他忙活的时候,两个青年民工进来争着与他一起干。就在他们争执的一瞬间,一块石头从洞壁上滚下来,砸在郭福贵的脚上,伤口流血不止。这是他第7次负伤了,他简单包扎了一下,又继续排除险石。当天晚上,他疼得一晚上没睡觉,第二天他又出现在了工地上,整整干了一天,收工时才被分指挥部领导发现。指挥部领导亲自送他去医院治疗,然而,第二天他却又跑回工地上了。家里孩子得了重病,妻子几次捎信让他回去,他给妻子带话说,工地很

Of the five adits that needed to be excavated, three were located in the middle of the high cliff. Here, the upper and lower parts of the high cliff were protruding, and the middle was concave, which was called "bending cliff". The workers fixed two steel chisels on the top of the cliff. A thick rope was tied to each steel chisel. Two blasters went down the cliff along the ropes to the elevation of the tunnel, drilled blast holes and then conducted blasting. The second commando team, with Guo Fugui as the team leader, was responsible for digging the second adit. He and two blasters went down the cliff from the top of the mountain, with ropes tied around their waists. When they looked down, the valley tens of feet deep made them dizzy. When they looked up, the huge rock overhead made them gasp for air. They were sometimes floating in the air like leaves, and sometimes clinging to the cliff like geckoes. Under the leadership of Guo Fugui, the second commando team, in the spirit of self-sacrifice, constantly hit steel chisels with hammers, advancing inch by inch to the depths of the mountain. After finishing work every day, he organized the team to summarize the construction experience of the day, find out problems, and encourage everyone to work out more ways to improve work efficiency. He was injured six times. After each injury, he endured the pain bravely and tried every means to keep secrets from his leaders so as not to leave the construction site. His back was wounded, and his leader found blood on his back and asked him what happened. He replied that he had a crusted tetter on his back and it didn't matter. One night, soon after a blasting in the tunnel, he was the first to enter the tunnel to remove dangerous rocks. With a lantern in one hand and a hammer in the other, he knocked off loose rocks one by one. While he was working, two young workers came in and scrambled to work with him. Just then, a stone rolled off the tunnel wall and hit Guo Fugui's foot. The wound was bleeding. It was the seventh time he had been injured, and he simply bandaged it and continued to remove the dangerous stones. That night, he couldn't sleep in pain all night. The next day, he appeared on the construction site again. He worked for a whole day and was only discovered by the leader of the branch command when he finished work. The leader personally took him to the hospital for treatment, but the next day he ran back to the construction site. On one occasion, his child was seriously ill, and his wife sent messages to him several times and asked him to go back home. He told his wife that he was very

忙，自己离不开，再说自己也不是医生，回家也给孩子治不了病，让妻子自己带孩子就近找个医生看看。他还担任着郭家窑大队队长，时间长了，大队有些事情需要他回去处理，他就当天下工后步行赶回去，办完事后，又连夜步行往工地赶，到达工地时，正好赶上大家早上出工。第4号旁洞的洞口位置在悬崖凹下去的地方，这一段是光溜溜的罗锅肚形，上没法上，下没法下，油光滑溜的岩壁上炸药根本放不上去。突击队长王秀松就带着人把炸药包绑在长长的杆子上，顶放在洞口位置上，一点一点地炸，等炸开一个工作面后，先上去一个人，在上面固定好一条绳子，其他人再攀着绳子上。

女民工同男民工一样，每天就这样爬上爬下。开挖出洞口后向里面掘进，每天都有规定的进度，而且奖罚严明，十二小时轮班倒。队长王秀松是一个很要强的人，提出了"红旗永驻西河连，坚决带水把家还"的口号。王爱莲、王华平姐妹俩人都是扶钎的好手，一人扶钎，四人打锤。一个女民工拇指被砸碎了，她硬是一声不吭地坚持到最后，后来她的这根指头变成了猴头指。

隧洞石质坚硬，一锤打下去，钢钎乱蹦，扶钎人被震得手臂发麻，而岩石上却只留下一个白点，10多根钢钎砸坏了都打不成一个炮眼。面对这种情况，卸甲坪连的炮手李王喜发明了立炮、连环炮等爆破技术。在工地上李王喜看谁打钎的姿势不对，或者打的炮眼定位错了，他都要严肃地指出来。哪一次爆破效果好，他就高兴得像个孩子似的，脸上笑成花儿；哪一炮没出力，效果差，他会懊恼半天。

busy at the construction site and couldn't leave, and besides, he was not a doctor and couldn't cure his child even if he went back home. He asked his wife to take the child to a doctor nearby. Meanwhile, he served as the leader of the Guojiayao production brigade. Sometimes, when the brigade needed him to deal with some matters, he would go back on foot after the day's work. After settling down the matters, he would walk back to the construction site overnight. When he arrived at the construction site, he was just in time for work in the morning. The opening of the fourth adit was located at the concave part of the cliff, which was very smooth and inaccessible to workers, and explosives could not be placed on it at all. The commando leader Wang Xiusong asked the workers to tie satchel charges to long poles and put them at the entrance of the adit, blasting rocks little by little. When a working face was formed, Wang Xiusong asked a worker to climb up first and fix a rope on it, and the others grabbed the rope and climbed up the cliff.

Female workers, like male workers, climbed up and down like this every day. After the excavation of the entrance, the workers started to dig inside, with a specified progress every day, strict rules of rewards and punishment, and 12-hour shifts. Wang Xiusong was a very competitive person and had put forward the slogan "The red flag is always flying in the Xihe Team and we are determined to bring water home". The sisters Wang Ailian and Wang Huaping were both good at holding steel chisels. One of them held the steel chisel while four workers took turns to hammer it. A female worker's thumb was smashed. She endured the pain without saying a word until the work was finished. Later, her thumb was left with permanent disability.

The rock in the tunnel was very hard, and when a hammer went down, the steel chisel bounced around. The chisel holder's arm was numb with shock, but only a white spot was left on the rock. More than 10 steel chisels were damaged, but no blast hole could be completed. In the face of this situation, Li Wangxi, the blaster of the Xiejiaping Team, invented such blasting technologies as vertical blasting and serial blasting. On the construction site, whenever Li Wangxi found that anyone was hammering in a wrong way or any blast hole was positioned incorrectly, he would point it out. When the blasting effect was good, he was as happy as a child with a smile on his face. When the blasting effect was poor, he would be chagrined for a long time.

虽然每天都是那样劳累、繁忙,但是每一个开凿青年洞的民工都坚信,最后、最美的巨变都将来自于日复一日的努力。他们坚持自己"把水带回家"的信念,每天都在为这个信念做出自己的贡献。在隧洞一寸一寸的掘进过程中,凿洞的智慧也在生长,他们实行双层施工,上层先推进,下层再挖底。在上层推进中,打出口小肚大的"瓦缸炮",当推进到一定深度时,再在下层打出两个平炮,利用上层的临空面,提高爆破效果。他们把下层的两个平炮叫作"抬炮"。上下层交替推进,瓦缸炮、抬炮交错爆破,掘进速度有所加快。

频繁的爆破,危险如影相随。在3号旁洞劳作的郭榜金与工友们从洞里出来,刚躲到安全的地方,就听见"轰"的一声炮响。他的第一反应就是出事了,根据他的经验,不该这么快就响炮,王保成、张学法、郭合章还在洞里查看线路呢。他们几人就往洞口跑,到了洞口,只见洞口像个大烟囱,硝烟滚滚直往外冒。他们试着往洞里冲,浓烟太大了,冲了几次都冲不进去。等烟稍散以后,他们立即进洞救人,洞里的烟依然很大,睁不开眼,几个人就手挽手,并排走着用脚趟着地找人。他们先用脚探着找到了张学法和郭合章,马上抬出洞外。两人都身负重伤,他们的衣服已被爆破所形成的冲击波撕得稀烂,身上布满了大大小小的石块,有的已插入肉中,还有半截露在外面。郭合章是郭榜金的族叔,他吃力地从口袋里掏出一个针线包还有一些粮票交给郭榜金,说自己恐怕活不了了,把这些东西交给郭榜金的奶奶。郭榜金顾不上安慰老叔,

Although they were so tired and busy every day, every worker who dug the Youth Tunnel was convinced that the last and most beautiful changes came from their day-to-day efforts. They always adhered to the belief of "bringing water home" and made their own contribution to this belief every day. In the process of tunneling inch by inch, the worker's wisdom in tunneling was also growing. They adopted a double-layer construction method, advancing the upper layer first, and then digging the lower layer. In the process of advancing the upper layer, the workers first carried out the "crock blasting" with small entrance and large middle space. When advancing to a certain depth, they carried out two horizontal blasting in the lower layer, using the free surface of the upper layer to improve the blasting effect. They called the horizontal blasting in the lower layer "lifting blasting". The upper and lower layers were pushed forward with "crock blasting" and "lifting blasting" alternately, thus accelerating the tunneling speed.

Frequent explosions were accompanied by danger. After finishing the work in the third adit, Guo Bangjin and his workmates came out of the tunnel. No sooner had they hidden themselves in a safe place than they heard a loud bang. His first reaction was that an accident happened. According to his experience, blasting shouldn't have started so quickly. Wang Baocheng, Zhang Xuefa and Guo Hezhang were still checking the wires in the tunnel. They ran to the entrance of the tunnel. When they got there, they saw that the entrance was like a big chimney, and the smoke billowed out of it. They tried to rush into the tunnel, but the smoke was so thick that they couldn't get in after a few rushes. After the smoke was slightly dispersed, they immediately went into the tunnel to rescue people. The smoke in the tunnel was still very thick, and they couldn't open their eyes. Therefore, they walked side by side, hand in hand, to search for people with their feet. They first found Zhang Xuefa and Guo Hezhang with their feet and immediately carried them out of the tunnel. Both men were seriously injured. Their clothes had been torn by the blasting shock wave. They were covered with big and small broken stones, some of which were inserted into their bodies with half exposed. Guo Hezhang, the uncle of Guo Bangjin, took out a sewing kit and some food coupons from his pocket with difficulty and handed them to Guo Bangjin, saying that he might not be able to live and asking Guo Bangjin to give them to his grandmother. Guo Bangjin had no time to comfort his uncle, and

就又与大家返回洞里，用同样的方法找到了王保成。然而，王保成在被抬出洞外不久就停止了呼吸。

隧洞凿到一定深度后，虽然点有几盏马灯，但光线依然朦胧昏暗。打平眼炮时，打钎和扶钎都得跪着。这种姿势使抡锤者很不好把握，经常打脱，砸到扶钎者的手臂上、肩上，疼得叫人哭笑不得。卸甲坪连的王来金面朝洞内跪着扶钎，由于光线昏暗，姿势难受，跪着抡锤的王明周，一锤砸在了王来金背上，王来金疼得半天说不出话来。女青年们也不示弱，卸甲坪连的铁姑娘李彩珍、李银花、靳雪英、王随新、张改娣5人一组，一人扶两根钎，供4人锻打。

连长马贵林带头实干，每天都是汗流浃背。他只顾干活，不顾身体，引发了哮喘、咳嗽不止，从没有休息过一晌。后来又得了胃溃疡，但他晚上仍带着民工加班到深夜，胃疼了，他就吃一把小苏打。他根据工程的进展，不断调整施工队伍。隧洞掘进到深处后，他将所有人员分为三拨：一拨主攻开挖；一拨清渣出渣；一拨清底，也就是把那些高出的硬鼓突炸平。目标节点化，节点责任化，每天的任务指标，不论多晚，都必须完成。

漳河库渠管理所副所长岳松栋是任村公社盘山村人，工地离他的家很近，但他与其他民工一样，日夜坚守在工地上，从不因住得近而顺便回家看看。他在凿洞中动脑筋、勤琢磨，而且善于总结经验，逐渐摸索、创造出了在工作面上布局"三角炮""拐弯炮"等爆破方法。这些

he ran into the tunnel with others and found Wang Baocheng in the same way. Unfortunately, Wang Baocheng stopped breathing shortly after being carried out of the tunnel.

After the tunnel was cut to a certain depth, although there were several lanterns, the light was still dim. When chiseling blast holes for horizontal blasting, the workers had to kneel down to work, whether with hammers or steel chisels. This posture made it difficult for the hammering man to keep his direction and often missed the target, hitting the arm and shoulder of the man holding the steel chisel, and thus injuring them. Wang Laijin of the Xiejiaping Team was kneeling down to hold the steel chisel. Due to the dim light and uncomfortable posture, Wang Mingzhou, hammering while kneeling down, hit Wang Laijin on the back with the hammer. Wang Laijin was so painful that he could not speak for a long time. The young women did not want to give the impression of weakness. Li Caizhen, Li Yinhua, Jin Xueying, Wang Suixin and Zhang Gaidi, the iron girls from the Xiejiaping Team, formed a group of five, one holding two steel chisels while the other four hammering.

The team leader Ma Guilin took the lead and worked hard every day. He only cared about his work and neglected his health, causing asthma. He often coughed, but he never took a day off. Later, he suffered from gastric ulcer. He still worked late into the night with the workers. When he felt a stomachache, he would eat a handful of baking soda. He often adjusted the construction team according to the progress of the project. After the tunnel was dug into the depths, he divided all the personnel into three groups: one focused on excavation, one cleared and removed the excavated material, and one cleared the bottom, that is, blasting out those protruding rocks. The target breakdown was made, with responsibility for each work. Every day, no matter how late it was, the task target must be completed.

Yue Songdong, deputy director of the Zhanghe Reservoir and Canal Management Office, was from Panshan Village of Rencun Commune. The construction site was very close to his home, but like other workers, he stayed on the construction site day and night, never going home. In the process of tunnel excavation, he often used his wits and was good at summing up experience. Gradually he invented blasting methods such as "triangle blasting" and "turning

岳松栋在讲解"三角炮"原理
Yue Songdong was explaining the method of "triangle blasting"

方法的使用使日凿洞推进由0.3米提高到1米、1.4米直到2.8米，极大地提高了工作效率。

良工谋事，玉汝于成。1961年7月15日，当清晨的阳光驱散笼罩在山间的迷雾，青年洞内卸甲坪连队的民工依稀听到了来自对面的声音。隧洞里顿时寂静下来，大家屏住呼吸，把耳朵贴在工作面上，倾听着、确认着，果然听到了那边的敲击声，隧洞里顿时沸腾了，梦寐以求的愿望实现了，能不高兴吗？人们忘记了饥饿、劳累，欢呼雀跃，奔走相告。连长马贵林赶紧派人把这个好消息传递给共同战斗的杨家窑连队。在距离隧洞开工一年零五个月的时候，开凿隧洞的民工在与岩石的对决

blasting". Due to the use of these methods, the tunneling speed was increased from 0.3 meter to 1 meter, 1.4 meters, 2.8 meters per day, greatly improving the working efficiency.

  A fine work entails a craftsman's utmost efforts and difficulty is the nurse of greatness. On July 15, 1961, when the early morning sun dispelled the fog shrouded in the mountains, the workers from the XieJiaping Team in the Youth Tunnel vaguely heard the voice from the opposite side. The people in the tunnel immediately fell silent. Everyone held their breath, put their ears on the working face, listened and confirmed. Indeed, they heard the knocking sound over there. The people in the tunnel immediately became overjoyed and their dream came true! How could they not be happy? People forgot hunger and fatigue, cheered and ran about to tell the news. Immediately, the team leader Ma Guilin sent people to pass the good news to the Yangjiayao team that was working together

中，从大山的肚子里掏出了15400立方米的土石方，这个横穿悬崖的隧洞终于打通了。

青年洞的竣工意味着整个红旗渠第二期工程完成了一半，更重要的是它打开了红旗渠通向林县腹地的门户。前面还有多少座高山挡路？总干渠还有多久才能通水？此时此刻，没有人再去考虑这些，所有的人只相信一个简单的道理，只要像青年洞这样不停地凿下去，渠，总有一天会修成的；水，总有一天会流过来的。

1961年11月30日，红旗渠第二期工程竣工，总干渠又向前延伸了10687米。从6月10日到11月30日，在苍茫的太行山上，历时半年，跨越寒暑，那么单调，那么漫长。修渠民工顶住了烈日，挡住了寒风，吞下了苦，咽下了痛，以顽强的姿态做工1681109个、开挖土石方588551立方米、砌筑125953立方米，任村公社6个村6100亩土地得到了灌溉，上万人吃水困难的问题得到了根本解决。

即将竣工的青年洞
The Youth Tunnel to be completed

with them. It had been one year and five months since the construction of the tunnel started. The workers had taken out 15,400 cubic meters of earth and stone from the belly of the mountain during the battle with the rocks. The tunnel crossing the cliff was finally completed.

The completion of the Youth Tunnel meant that the second phase of the Hongqiqu Canal was completed in half. More importantly, it opened the passage of the Hongqiqu Canal to the hinterland of Linxian County. How many more mountains were still standing in the way? How long would it take for the General Main Canal to transfer water? At this moment, no one was thinking about these problems any more. All the people believed in a simple truth: As long as you kept excavating like in the Youth Tunnel, the canal would be completed one day and the water would come.

On November 30, 1961, the second phase of the Hongqiqu Canal was completed and the General Main Canal was extended forward by 10,687 meters. From June 10 to November 30, the workers spent half a year on the boundless Taihang Mountains. Enduring scorching sunlight, cold wind, hardship and pain with indomitable attitude, the workers completed 1,681,109 man-days, and carried out excavation of 588,551 cubic meters and masonry of 125,953 cubic meters. Over 400 hectares of farmland were irrigated in 6 villages of Rencun Commune, and the problem of drinking water for tens of thousands of people was fundamentally solved.

隔"三"修"四"

1961年8月的林县，干旱将高粱、玉米、谷子、红薯、豆角置于窘迫的山野，烈日炙烤，秸秆半枯，一切庄稼在绝望中挣扎。如何缓解当前的干旱困境？红旗渠第三期工程亟待提前布局、超前谋划。规划长度为70公里的总干渠已经通水20公里，10公里长的第二期工程再有两个多月也将竣工。按照原定计划，剩下的这40公里又分为第三期和第四期这两期来完成，第三期从木家庄到南谷洞，第四期从南谷洞到分水岭。如果按既定计划，正常情况下修完这40公里最少也得3年的时间，但是残酷的现实并没有给林县人民留下这么多时间，怎样才能尽快地让远水解近渴呢？

此时，库容达6900万立方米的南谷洞水库已蓄满了水，如果先修南谷洞至分水岭的第四期工程，可以把南谷洞水库的水引入林县腹地，这样就能够缓解部分公社的土地旱情。因长期艰苦的施工，群众总是得不到奋斗的收获，修渠的热情自然就会下降。如果调整一下施工顺序，先修第四期工程，可以让人民群众更早地从红旗渠的修建中获益，可以稳定群众情绪，激发全县人民更高的修渠热情。林县县委决定打破常规，从低垂的果实摘起，来一个"隔三修四"，让南谷洞水库通过红旗渠第四期工程的修建，早日发挥效用。

总干渠第四期工程是与第二期工程统一调度、交叉施工、压茬推进的，哪个公社先完成第二期工程哪个就先转移到第四期工程。1961年8

Constructing "the Fourth Phase" before "the Third Phase"

In August 1961, the drought in Linxian County put sorghums, corns, millets, sweet potatoes and beans in embarrassed fields. Under the scorching sun, the straws were half withered and all crops struggled in despair. How could they alleviate the current drought? The third phase of the Hongqiqu Canal project was in urgent need of layout and planning in advance. Out of the planned length of 70 kilometers of the General Main Canal, 20 kilometers had come into operation, and 10 kilometers of the second phase would be completed in more than two months. According to the original plan, the remaining 40 kilometers would be completed in two phases: the third phase would be from Mujiazhuang to Nangudong, and the fourth phase would be from Nangudong to the watershed. According to the established plan, it would normally take at least 3 years to complete the 40 kilometers, but the cruel reality did not leave so much time for the people of Linxian County. How could they make the distant water quench the present thirst as soon as possible?

At this time, the Nangudong Reservoir with a storage of 69 million cubic meters was full of water. If the fourth phase of the project from Nangudong to the watershed was completed first, the water from the Nangudong Reservoir could be transferred into the hinterland of Linxian County, thus alleviating the drought in some communes. Due to long-term and arduous construction without reaping the fruits of the struggle, the local people's enthusiasm to construct the canal would naturally decline. If the construction sequence was adjusted and the fourth phase of the project was built first, the local people could benefit earlier from the construction of the Hongqiqu Canal, their mood could be stabilized, and higher enthusiasm of the whole county for canal construction could be generated. The Linxian County Party Committee decided to change the original plan and construct the fourth phase before the third phase so that Nangudong Reservoir could play its role as soon as possible.

The fourth phase and the second phase of the General Main Canal would be uniformly controlled, cross-constructed and steadily promoted. The commune that completed the second phase first would transfer to the fourth phase first. On

月26日，河顺、采桑、合涧、小店4个公社的6个连队先行转移到第四期工地上了。10月6日，这4个公社的民工全部转入第四期工程施工。第四期工程就是这样由先后完成第二期工程任务的连队转移下来再陆续开始施工的。

红旗渠寄托着林县人民对美好生活的追求和向往。自工程开工以来，全县人民只专注做一件事，就是瞄准"引漳入林"这个突破口发起冲锋。在那段时间里，修渠作为一种制度性安排，已经成为林县人生活的一部分，需要谁上修渠工地，哪怕这个人正在家里吃饭，也要放下饭碗背起工具赶往工地。临走时村里人还会叮嘱："好好干，别给咱村丢人！"那些在外工作回乡探亲的人，在休探亲假期间也有人会去工地上干上一阵子。从县、公社到大队，各级组织对红旗渠建设十分关心，只要是红旗渠工地上有需要，县直各部门会全力解决，各公社会不断派人到工地上慰问并全力支持红旗渠建设，要人给人，要物给物。为了让红旗渠早日通水，后方倾力支持，前方奋发努力。工地上各公社、各连队的民工都是你追我赶赛进度，争先恐后比质量，千方百计保安全。

全长115米的桑耳庄隧洞，由小店公社的南山、鹤山、平家辛庄、北马巷4个连队的130名民工负责开凿。该隧洞地质条件很差，顶部厚度达16米，全部都是土夹石，黏结度差。隧洞中间还有一道天然裂隙，开洞过程中，虚土不停地往下塌，施工时只能边塌边挖，进度很慢。

1961年一冬无雪，大雪却在1962年的春天赶来了。1962年2月24

August 26, 1961, six teams of the four communes of Heshun, Caisang, Hejian and Xiaodian moved to the construction site of the fourth phase. On October 6, all the workers of the four communes were transferred to the fourth phase. All parts of the fourth phase were started successively by the workers who had already completed the second phase and been transferred here.

The Hongqiqu Canal embodied the Linxian People's pursuit and yearning for a better life. Since the start of the project, the people of the whole county only focused on one thing, namely the goal of "channeling the Zhanghe River into Linxian County". During that period, the canal construction, as an institutional arrangement, became a part of the people's life in Linxian County. Whoever was needed to go to the canal construction site, no matter what he was doing, must take up his tools and rush to the construction site. When he left, the villagers would also tell him, "Do a good job and don't embarrass our village!" When those who worked outside their hometown returned home on vacation, they would also go to the construction site and work for a while. From the county, a commune to a brigade, Party committees at all levels were very concerned about the construction of the Hongqiqu Canal. As long as there was a need on the construction site, all departments of the county government would do their best to meet it. Every commune would send people to the construction site to extend regards and fully supported the construction of the Hongqiqu Canal, providing manpower and materials. In order to complete the Hongqiqu Canal as soon as possible, all the people outside the construction site gave their full support and the workers on the construction site competed with each other to speed up the project progress, and did everything possible to pursue good quality and ensure the safety of construction.

The 115-meter-long Sangerzhuang Tunnel was excavated by 130 workers from four teams in Xiaodian Commune, namely Nanshan, Heshan, Pingjiaxinzhuang and Beimaxiang. The geological conditions of the tunnel were very poor. The thickness of the tunnel top was 16 meters, consisting of earth mixed with stones. So, the cohesion was poor. There was a natural crack in the middle of the tunnel. In the process of excavation, loose earth kept falling down, which slowed down the progress.

There was no snow in the winter of 1961, but heavy snow came in the spring

劈山导河
Tunneling the mountain and diverting the river

日,鹅毛般的大雪在灰暗的天空中飞舞,露天施工被迫暂停了,隧洞内则继续施工。3月2日,总指挥长马有金来到桑耳庄隧洞施工现场。隧洞已经开凿4个月了,还剩最后的36米没有凿通,关键是洞内那个天然裂缝,塌方严重,向前掘进异常困难。马有金召集分指挥部和连队领导、工地技术人员、民工代表共同研究战胜裂缝塌方的办法。大家提出了两个方案:一是继续凿洞,但要拐个弯,绕开裂缝;另一种方案是废弃现有隧洞,绕山修明渠。如果按第一个方案,绕过裂缝,继续凿洞的话,还需用1万个工,工期会延长;如果采用第二个方案,绕山修明渠的话,渠道要延长1500米,还要再用5万个工,同时意味着前面4个月的努力就前功尽弃了,而且还要多占用耕地并会毁掉很多树木,工期同样

of 1962. On February 24, 1962, heavy snowfall fluttered like goose feathers in the gray sky, which forced the open-air construction to be suspended while the construction continued inside the tunnel. On March 2, Ma Youjin, the General Commander, came to the construction site of the Sangerzhuang Tunnel. The tunnel had been excavated for 4 months, and the last 36 meters had not been excavated. The problem was that the natural crack in the tunnel seriously collapsed and it was extremely difficult to advance. Ma Youjin convened leaders of the branch command, team leaders, site technicians, and representatives of workers to jointly study ways to solve the problem of crack landslides. Two plans were put forward: one was to continue to excavate the tunnel, but turn a corner to avoid the crack; the other plan was to abandon the existing tunnel and build an open canal along the mountain. According to the first plan, if the crack was bypassed to continue the excavation of the tunnel, it would take another 10,000 man-days and the construction period would be prolonged. If the second plan was adopted to build the open canal along the mountain, the canal would be extended by 1,500 meters and another 50,000 man-days would be required, which also meant that the efforts made in the previous four months would be wasted, more farmland

也会延长。经过反复对比，马有金与大家商定采用第一个方案，绕过裂缝继续凿洞。在施工方法上每掘进2米就停下来进行垒砌、砌拱券，然后再往前掘进，如次循环往复，以保证开凿的协调、安全。桑耳庄隧洞内的民工昼夜不停，分班轮战，在双孔隧洞上又开了两个旁洞，四处齐攻，六面放炮，这个长115米、单孔高4.5米、宽4米的复杂顽固的双孔隧洞，最终顺利竣工。

分水岭是漳河与洹河的分界线，由于岭上古坟较多，当地人也称"坟头岭"。要想让漳河水通过，必须在岭下10~15米深处挖凿一个长240米的隧洞。林县人千百年来想漳河水、盼漳河水，就是因为通不过这个岭而望水兴叹。要在这里开凿隧洞，首先要在隧洞两端同时开挖一条总长100米，深、宽各10米的深沟明渠。在隧洞施工中，因岩石破碎塌方，将原设计的孔径为7米的单孔洞改为孔径3.5米的双孔洞，以改善洞顶受力条件。凿洞的民工采取边开挖、边砌衬的方法，避免洞内塌方。由于该隧洞正处于山体的断裂带上，整个洞体大都是土夹石，黏结性差，一挖就塌方，进度慢、工效低。这个隧洞是总干渠的结尾工程，尽快凿通，可以尽快让南谷洞水库早日发挥效益，早日造福岭南的群众，这个隧洞也是全县人民的"希望洞"。总指挥部从姚村、泽下、原康、采桑选调技术好的石匠，将隧洞两端高10米的渠墙进行了衬砌。为了节省土地，在衬砌的基础上，又把部分明渠进行石头券砌，改为暗渠，洞上覆土为田，隧洞最终延长为354米。

would be occupied, many trees would be destroyed, and the construction period would also be extended. After repeated comparisons, everyone agreed to adopt the first plan, bypassing the crack and continuing the tunneling. In terms of the construction method, excavation would be stopped every 2 meters to carry out the lining, and then the excavation would go on. Thus, the coordination and safety of the excavation could be ensured. The workers in the Sangerzhuang Tunnel worked round the clock in shifts. They dug two adits in the double-hole tunnel, so that the tunnel could be excavated in four places and blasted in six places. Finally, the complex and stubborn double-hole tunnel, 115 meters long, 4.5 meters high and 4 meters wide, was successfully completed.

The watershed was the dividing line between the Zhanghe River and the Huanhe River. Because there were many ancient tombs in the mountain, the local people also called it the "Tomb Ridge". In order to allow the water of the Zhanghe River to pass through, a 240-meter-long tunnel must be excavated 10~15 meters below the ridge. The people of Linxian County had been looking forward to the water of the Zhanghe River for thousands of years, but the water could not pass through this mountain ridge. To excavate a tunnel here, a deep channel with a total length of 100 meters, a depth of 10 meters and a width of 10 meters should be excavated first at both ends of the tunnel. During the tunnel construction, due to rock breakage and collapse, the designed single-hole tunnel with a diameter of 7 meters was changed to a double-hole tunnel with a diameter of 3.5 meters to improve the stress conditions on the roof of the tunnel. The workers adopted the method of digging and lining at the same time to avoid collapse. As the tunnel was located on the fault zone of the mountain, the working area was mostly earth mixed with stones, with poor cohesiveness, frequent landslides, slow progress and low work efficiency. This tunnel was the ending project of the General Main Canal. Its earlier completion would enable the Nangudong Reservoir to benefit the people in the south of the ridge as soon as possible. This tunnel was also the "Hope Tunnel" of the entire county. The General Command chose skilled stonemasons from Yaocun, Zexia, Yuankang and Caisang to build the 10-meter-high walls at both ends of the tunnel. In order to save farmland, the open channels were covered with arch top, above which, the backfill was changed into fields. Therefore, the tunnel was extended to 354 meters.

分水岭隧洞施工
The construction of watershed tunnel

　　1962年10月15日，总干渠第四期工程竣工，南谷洞水库下泄的清流翻滚着白色的浪花，畅通无阻地穿越分水岭隧洞，沿着太行山西侧临时开通的渠道向南流去。渠道沿线的群众看到红旗渠水从村前流过，感觉像在做梦一样，有点不敢相信自己的眼睛，但它却真实地存在。他们真切地感受到，横跨太行山直达林县的那条天河，真的出现了，再也不是可望而不可及的梦幻。

On October 15, 1962, the fourth phase of the General Main Canal was completed. The clear water discharged from the Nangudong Reservoir passed through the watershed tunnel, flowing southward along the temporarily constructed canal on the west side of the Taihang Mountains. Seeing the water of the Hongqiqu Canal flowing by their village, the local people felt like they were dreaming and couldn't believe their eyes, but it was real. They truly felt that the Heavenly River, which crossed the Taihang Mountains and directly reached Linxian County, really appeared, and it was no longer an elusive dream.

漳河水来了

1962年10月20日，红旗渠总干渠的最后一期工程拉开了帷幕。把最后一段渠道贯通，漳河水就会进入干旱的林县。

渠道一来到盘阳，被一道高山拦腰挡住，只有钻一个长240米、高4.7米、宽6米的隧洞，水才能流过去。山是火炼石，坚硬似铁，全靠一锤锤敲打，一炮炮崩炸，炮小了工效低，炮大了容易塌方。当隧洞挖掘到30米深时，采桑公社南采桑连负责的西洞口突然发生了冒顶事故。洞顶上塌下来齐腰深的石方，堵住了施工断面。公社分指挥长郭增堂来到西洞口，只见洞顶上还在不断往下落石块。他对垂头丧气的南采桑连长宋榜吉说："现在不是愁眉苦脸的时候，需要的是动脑筋，想办法，给大家出主意。"宋榜吉却说："咱绕道修明渠吧，修明渠虽然费点工，民工不冒险，咱当干部的也不担心，还能按时通水。"旁边的民工也都表示同意宋榜吉的意见。是排险除难继续钻洞，还是前功尽弃另修明渠，这样两难的选择摆在郭增堂面前。他没有武断地下命令，而是让大家比较凿隧洞与修明渠的利弊。经过权衡，大家终于认识到在这里修明渠弊大于利：渠线距盘阳村非常近，要修渠必然要占用地、毁坏树木，放炮作业还会危及盘阳村群众的生命和财产安全，综合来看还是凿隧洞更为有利。

根据纽约帝国大厦设计师的说法，建筑是和平时期最为接近战争的活动。那么修渠就是打仗，凿洞就是进攻敌人碉堡。碉堡里的"敌

The Water from the Zhanghe River Is Coming

On October 20, 1962, the people of Linxian County started the construction of the final phase of the Hongqiqu General Main Canal. Once the last section of the canal was completed, the water from the Zhanghe River would enter the dry land of Linxian County.

When the canal came to Panyang Village, it was blocked by a mountain. A tunnel 240 meters long, 4.7 meters high and 6 meters wide must be excavated. The mountain stone was as hard as iron. The excavation only relied on hammers and blasting. The efficiency would be low with small blasting while collapse would happen with big blasting. When the tunnel was excavated to a depth of 30 meters, a sudden collapse occurred in the west portal, where the Nancaisang construction team of Caisang Commune was working. The stones that collapsed down blocked the construction section. Guo Zengtang, the Branch Commander of the commune, came to the site and saw stones still falling from the tunnel roof. He said to Song Bangji, the downhearted Nancaisang team leader, that what was needed right now was to work out a solution, not to wear a worried look. Song Bangji suggested constructing an open canal. Although it might take more manpower, the workers would not take risks, the leaders would not have to worry, and what's more, the canal could release water on time. The workers around also agreed to Song Bangji's suggestion. It was a dilemma for Guo Zengtang whether to overcome difficulties to continue the tunnel or to build an open canal with all their previous efforts wasted. He did not make arbitrary orders, but let them compare the advantages and disadvantages of a tunnel and an open canal. On balance, it was realized that there were more disadvantages to build an open canal here: the canal line was close to Panyang Village, the construction of an open canal would occupy the farmland and destroy the trees, and the blasting operation would also endanger the villagers and their property. On the whole, it was more advantageous to excavate a tunnel.

According to the designer of the Empire State Building in New York, the architecture is the closest thing to war in peacetime. Then, to build the canal was to fight, and to excavate the tunnel was to attack the enemy's blockhouse. The "enemy" in the blockhouse was very tenacious and the leaders needed to take the

人"很顽强，需要领导干部带头冲进去。采桑分指挥部30名干部组成的突击队，要首先冲进塌方的隧洞。分指挥长郭增堂扶了扶安全帽，第一个钻进洞里。蛮横遇上了刚强，这支干部突击队冒着塌方的风险，要为隧洞的施工开辟出一条通路。他们用铁钩把洞顶上的活动险石一块块地勾掉，又一筐筐地抬出。郭增堂手磨破了，肩压肿了，寒湿侵袭着他那瘦瘦的身体，他忍受着浑身关节的疼痛，坚持在洞内施工。半个月过去了，突击队清除险石160多立方米，直到为民工开辟出一条安全施工通道才撤出。安全通道修好了，南采桑连的民工们的顾虑消除了，隧洞的施工又恢复了。吝惜汗水和力量，哪一条路都是弯路；朝着目标努力，整个世界都会为你让路。

  红旗渠第三期工程与浊河的尾部相遇了。浊河从山西省平顺县的虹梯关流下，这里的河床经过洪水数千年的冲刷下切，形成了深深的峡谷。河床坡降较陡，汛期一涨二三里，来势凶猛，裹挟着大量泥沙、卵石顺流而下。当百年一遇的洪水发生时流量高达1500立方米/秒，而枯水期时又缩成一道细流，稍一干旱就枯竭断流。这种不规律的水文特征使得大量卵石在河床淤积，河床上卵石层最厚处达40米，浅处也有20米。红旗渠无论如何也无法摆脱它的山高谷深，建设者们必须找到一种新方法让渠水不犯河水，让它们各行其道。起初，设计者们先是考虑在浊河汇入露水河的河口处建一座长570米、高14米、内宽6米的渡槽，让洪水从渡槽下泄走。这是一个渠线最短、水头损失最小的方案，但问题来了：一是该处地基不良，下挖卵石层至少20米，而且安全很难保

lead. 30 leaders in the Caisang Branch Command formed a commando team to rush into the collapsed tunnel. The Branch Commander Guo Zengtang was the first to enter the tunnel. The team risked collapse and opened up a path for the construction of the tunnel. They removed the dangerous stones overhead with iron hooks, and carried them out of the tunnel with baskets. Guo Zengtang's hands were worn, his shoulders were swollen, and his thin body suffered from the cold-dampness. He endured the pain of his joints and insisted on working in the tunnel. Half a month later, the commando team cleared more than 160 cubic meters of dangerous stones until a safe passage was opened up for the workers. The safe passage relieved the concerns of the workers of the Nancaisang construction team, and the tunnel construction was restored. If one spared his effort, every road was a detour; if one worked towards the goal and the whole world would make way for him.

The third phase of the Hongqiqu Canal met the tail of the Zhuohe River. The Zhuohe River flowed from the Hongtiguan Pass in Pingshun County of Shanxi Province. The riverbed here was washed and cut for thousands of years, forming a deep canyon. The slope of the riverbed was steep, and in the rainy season, the flooding was fierce, carrying a large number of silt and pebbles downstream. When a once-in-a-century flood occurred, the flow rate was as high as 1,500 cubic meters per second. However, in the dry season, the river shrank into a thin stream and the slightest drought would dry up the flow. This irregular hydrological feature caused a large number of pebbles to deposit on the riverbed, with a maximum thickness of 40 meters and a minimum thickness of 20 meters. In any case, the Hongqiqu Canal could not avoid high mountains and deep valleys. The builders had to find a new way to ensure that the canal would not violate the river and both could go their own way. At first, the designers considered constructing an aqueduct, 570 meters long, 14 meters high and 6 meters wide, at the estuary where the Zhuohe River emptied into the Lushuihe River, allowing the flood to escape under the aqueduct. It was a scheme with the shortest canal route and the least water head loss, but there were problems. Firstly, the foundation was poor, with the pebble layer at least 20 meters thick, and the safety was difficult to guarantee. Secondly, the construction was very difficult to execute since huge amounts of materials were required for the construction and it was necessary to

证；二是工程所需建筑材料数量庞大，又要高空作业，施工难度高；三是渡槽的南端直抵白家庄村，必须拆迁移民，无形中增加了工程造价。总的来讲，采用这个方案就是投工、投资多，工期长，不可预测因素多。而且在当时技术水平、物质条件、工期要求的制约下，该方案难以实施。此路不通，只好另辟蹊径。设计者们又考虑了一个涵洞方案，总干渠由浊河河口处顺山逆河而行，达到渠道低于河底一定高度时，修建一座长1500米的双孔涵洞，渠水从洞中流过，洪水仍从原河道泄走。涵洞与渡槽相比，施工操作较为简便易行，但却要增加2830米渠线，并且如何防止涵洞进出口明渠段被洪水漫入和山前堆积物坍塌堵塞渠道这两个问题，没有很好的解决办法。如果将这段明渠改为暗渠，又增加了工程量，最后的结局就是工程量太大，投资、投工太多，极不经济。经过多番论证和比较，设计者从迫切需要解决的问题出发，最后决定采用空心坝方案。这一方案就是在浊河口左岸绕行到渠底与河底基本相平的地方，修建一条浆砌石空心溢流坝，使渠水由坝心涵洞流过，洪水从坝顶溢走。空心坝方案避免了高空作业，节约了大量石材，扩大了施工基础面，改善了地基的承载状况，克服了地基不良的缺点。而且工作面开阔，可以充分发挥人力资源优势，加快施工进度。与其他方案相比，这一方案在投工、投资、用料和工期等方面都比较经济、有利，而且技术上更加可靠，是破解河渠交汇难题的有效办法。

　　善筑者先清其基。在砂卵石覆盖层很厚的河床上挖掘空心坝基础，

work high above the ground. Thirdly, the southern end of the aqueduct directly reached Baijiazhuang Village, which would give rise to the resettlement of the villagers and inevitably increase the construction cost. In general, this scheme would lead to more cost, longer construction period, and more unpredictable factors. Moreover, due to the constraints of the present technology of the time, the material conditions and the construction period, this scheme was difficult to implement. Therefore, the designers worked out a new solution, a culvert. From the mouth of the Zhuohe River, the General Main Canal would go upstream along the mountain. When the canal reached a certain height below the riverbed, a two-hole culvert 1,500 meters long was to be built. The canal water would flow through the culvert and the floodwater would still flow through the original river channel. Compared with the aqueduct, the culvert was simple and easy to operate, but the canal length had to be increased by 2,830 meters, and there was no good solution to prevent the floodwater from entering the open canal sections at both ends of the culvert, and the debris piled by the mountain from collapsing and blocking the canal. If this section of the open canal was changed to a culvert, the work quantities would be increased, which would cause too much investment and labor, and would be extremely uneconomical. After many arguments and comparisons, the designers finally decided to construct a hollow dam. It was proposed to build the canal along the left bank of the Zhuohe River estuary and construct a masonry hollow overflow dam where the bottom of the canal and the riverbed were basically on the same level so that the canal water would flow through the dam culvert and the flood would flow over the dam crest. The hollow dam scheme avoided working high above the ground, saved a lot of stones, expanded the construction space, improved the bearing condition of the foundation, and overcame the shortcomings of poor foundation. Moreover, the work site was very open, and the advantages of human resources could be fully utilized to speed up the construction progress. Compared with other schemes, this scheme was economical and beneficial in terms of manpower, investment, materials and construction period, and technically more rcliable. It was an effective way to solve the intersection problem of the river and the canal.

The foundation clearing was essential for good construction. The excavation of the hollow dam foundation on a riverbed with a thick sandy gravel covering

遇到了很多过去从未遇到的难题。要在渠线底部下挖2米，这里既有流沙层，又有潜水层，导致前边刚开挖出渠基，后边就被流沙淤积了。在这里施工急不得更慢不得，只有边挖边设小堰阻挡流沙，同时快速排水，水排干后，工匠紧接着用水泥砂浆垒砌。各个工种同时操作，紧密配合，哪一项赶不上就会导致前功尽弃。

工程所需石料量很大，姚村公社爆破能手常根虎就在附近的山头上炸山开石。在一座山崖上有一条崖缝，是个很好的炮位，常根虎就带领几个民工从崖缝中凿了一个纵深8米、宽5米的大炮眼，装填炸药750公斤、煤500公斤。一炮就崩下1.1万立方米的石方，这就解决了一半的工程石料。但另一半上哪里找呢？常根虎又攀上另一侧山崖，发现这一侧山崖因长期受雨水冲刷，崖边伸出去的崖嘴上大下小，底部已与山体之间分离了，只有很少一部分连接着，孤悬一线。如果在这个山嘴底部放一炮，炸下这块崖嘴石，就可解决另一半石料问题。他带着4个民工来到崖嘴顶上，先贴着崖壁放下一条粗绳，叫作溜索，起保险作用，再把另一条绳子系在腰上，带上除险钩杆下崖了。当下到距崖顶40米时，他发现在崖壁凹进去的地方有个天然岩洞，可利用其作为炮洞。他的身体离洞口还有大约5米的距离，常根虎用除险的钩杆一顶崖壁，身体向外荡去，当身体再次荡回崖壁时，他借着惯性，顺势荡进了岩洞里。他在崖顶其他人员的配合下，将400公斤炸药装进了8米深的岩洞里。一炮过后，又得到了1万立方米的石料。

根据施工方案，坝体砌筑分两期进行，第一期先砌筑60米长。坝体临水面采用1米厚的水泥砂浆砌石块，中间用水泥砂浆填心。整个工程

encountered many problems never met before. The foundation shall be excavated for two meters under the canal, where both drift sand formation and phreatic water layer were encountered, which caused the foundation to be silted up by quicksand soon after it was excavated. The excavation here could not be carried out either in a hurry or slowly, but be executed with the construction of coffer dams to stop quicksand, and at the same time, the water was drained quickly and then the craftsmen completed the wet masonry immediately. All the departments operated at the same time and cooperated with each other closely. Any delay would lead to all the previous efforts wasted.

Stones were required for the project in large quantity. Chang Genhu, the blasting expert of Yaocun Commune, looked for stones in the nearby mountains. There was a crack in a cliff, which was a good position for blasting. Chang Genhu and several workers excavated a large blast hole, 8 meters deep and 5 meters wide, in the crack. 750 kilograms of explosives and 500 kilograms of coal were filled into the blast hole. 11,000 cubic meters of stone were mined with one blasting, which satisfied half of the total requirement. But where would they find the other half? Chang Genhu climbed to the cliff top from the other side of the mountain and found that the huge cliff top stretched outward due to rain wash and the lower part was separated from the mountain except a small part. One blasting at the lower part would blow down the cliff, and the other half of the stone problem would be solved. He led four workers to the top of the cliff, lowered a thick rope down the cliff as a protector, tied another rope to his waist and climbed down the cliff with a hook rod in his hand. When he lowered 40 meters from the cliff top, he found a natural cave in the recessed corner of the cliff, which could be used as a blast hole. When his body was about 5 meters away from the cave, Chang Genhu pushed the cliff hard with his hook rod to swing himself away, and when he swung back, he entered the cave by inertia. With the cooperation of other people at the top of the cliff, he loaded 400 kilograms of explosives into the 8-meter-deep cave. After a blasting, 10,000 cubic meters of stone were gained.

According to the construction plan, the dam masonry was carried out in two phases. The first phase was 60 meters. The upstream surface of the dam was made of 1-meter-thick cement mortar masonry, with cement mortar filled in the middle. The whole structure was basically wet masonry. The mortar placing

的垒砌基本上是浆砌片石,铺浆挤浆皆有讲究,通过用锤敲打使石料与砂浆紧密结合,而灰缝不得大于2厘米。砂浆所用的沙料必须是沙质坚硬、锐利富有棱角,不得掺有杂草、树根等杂质。分指挥长郭百锁不敢有半点放松,时刻在工地盯着,有病也坚持在工地上,民工们劝他回驻地休息,他说不亲眼看着不放心。总指挥马有金每天都要来工地查看,他手拿钢撬,不时地把砌好的片石撬开进行抽查,看石料底部是否座足了砂浆。坝是空心坝,但砌体不能空心化。砌石的工匠们每砌好一块石料,都要用钢撬插入石缝摇晃一下,看是否牢固,确保砌体不空心。

空心坝的建设共挖砌土石方2.2万立方米,投工15万个,建成了底宽20米、长166米的弓形坝体,坝腹有两个孔眼,孔宽3米,高4.5米,可承受流量为1500立方米/秒的洪水。1964年10月24日工程全部竣工。空心坝弓形坝体在增强抵御上游水压能力的同时,又使溢下的洪水流向

空心坝
The hollow dam

and filling required skills, with stones hammered to combine with mortar tightly, and joints less than 2 centimeters. The sand used in the mortar must be hard and angular, without any foreign matters such as weeds and roots. Guo Baisuo, the Branch Commander, did not dare to relax. He was always on the construction site, even when he was sick. The workers advised him to return to take a rest, but he said that he did not feel at ease without seeing the site. Ma Youjin, the General Commander, visited the construction site every day. From time to time, he pried the stones open to see if the bottom of the stone was filled with enough cement mortar. The dam was a hollow dam, but the masonry could not be hollow. Every time a masonry craftsman placed a piece of stone, he would insert a steel lever into the joint and shake it to see if the stone was firm and ensure that the masonry was not hollow.

For the construction of the hollow dam, 22,000 cubic meters of excavation and masonry were completed, and 150,000 man-days were used. The arch dam with a bottom width of 20 meters and a length of 166 meters had two holes in it, 3 meters wide and 4.5 meters high each. It could withstand a flood flow of 1,500 cubic meters per second. It was completed on October 24, 1964. The hollow arch dam enhanced the ability to withstand the upstream water pressure, and made the overflowing flood flow to the middle of the riverbed, which protected the open

河床中部，保护了两侧河岸上的明渠，还使坝心的涵洞与进出口渠道平顺地联结起来。坝腹的输水洞采用双孔拱形结构，降低了坝体高度，有效减小了河水对坝体的冲击。浊河很长，红旗渠也很长，林县人民让它们在这里完成历史与现实的交汇，一个渠水不犯河水的传奇故事就这样写进了红旗渠建设史。

露水河从远古风尘中一路走来，在山西高原的东部边缘横切太行山，形成了一条深切大峡谷。露水河在走出大峡谷时遇到了巨厚的石英砂岩层，所幸的是在这厚厚的石英岩下部恰巧发育了一层紫红色的黏土岩，在水流的侵蚀作用下，这层黏土岩被掏空，其上覆盖的坚硬石英砂岩被悬空。由于石英砂岩中垂直节理比较发育，而且这些垂直节理连通性又非常好，在地震、暴雨等外力诱发下沿垂直节理面发生崩塌。无数次的崩塌便形成了这段近一公里长，两岸石壁直立、河槽狭窄得像一条胡同似的河道，当地人称这种地形为谷洞。出谷洞后，河槽展宽，岸坡逐渐平缓，接纳西北方向来的支流浊河后，露水河继续向漳河流去。

红旗渠渠水从谷洞的西侧流过来，必须经过一座立体交叉建筑物，才能跨越露水河继续前进。一座长133米，底宽11.3米，高12米，由10孔石拱构成的渡槽就要在这里诞生。这座渡槽的特殊性就在于槽体要承受红旗渠25立方米/秒的水量的压力，槽墩还要顶住露水河1000立方米/秒最大泄洪水量的冲击。

茶店公社的民工在河道上边开挖墩基，边放炮从崖壁上崩下大堆的石块，用作砌筑渡槽的石料。这个公社位于林县南部山区，属于石灰岩构造，他们祖祖辈辈同石灰石打交道，经验丰富。而这里却是石英砂

canal on the river banks, and also smoothly connected the culverts in the dam with the canal. The culverts in the dam were two arch holes, which reduced the height of the dam and in turn the impact force of the river water on the dam. The Zhuohe River was very long, and the Hongqiqu Canal was also very long. The people of Linxian County let them complete the intersection of history and reality here. The legendary story that the canal did not offend the river was written into the history of the construction of the Hongqiqu Canal.

The Lushuihe River came all the way from the ancient times, and cut across the Taihang Mountains on the eastern edge of the Shanxi plateau, forming a deep canyon. The Lushuihe River encountered a thick quartz sandstone layer as it flowed out of the grand canyon. Fortunately, a layer of purple-red clay rock developed in the lower part of the quartz sandstone layer. Under the erosion of water, the clay rock was hollowed out and the hard quartz sandstone was suspended above. The quartz sandstone, in which the vertical joints were relatively developed and passed through the whole layer, collapsed along the vertical joints, induced by external forces such as earthquakes and heavy rains. Numerous times of collapse formed this section of riverbed, nearly one kilometer long, with upright cliffs on both banks and river channel as narrow as an alley. The locals called this terrain a valley tunnel. Out of the valley, the river channel widened and the bank slope gradually became flat. Joining the Zhuohe River coming from the northwest, the Lushuihe River continued to go to the Zhanghe River.

The Hongqiqu Canal came from the west side of the valley and had to cross the Lushuihe River through a flyover building to continue the journey. An aqueduct would be born here, 133 meters long, 11.3 meters wide and 12 meters high, with 10 stone arches. This aqueduct must withstand the water flow of 25 cubic meters per second in the Hongqiqu Canal, and the piers must withstand the impact of the maximum discharge of 1,000 cubic meters per second in the Lushuihe River.

The workers of Chadian Commune excavated the pier foundation on the riverbed, and blasted quartz sandstone from the cliffs for the construction of the aqueduct. This commune was located in the southern mountainous area of Linxian County and its geology belonged to limestone structure. The workers had rich experience with limestone for generations, but here was quartz sandstone.

岩，工地上50多名石匠锻打石灰石不在话下，但要对付这种比石灰岩坚硬得多的石英砂岩却是个棘手的问题。但民工们不等不靠，一切自己摸索，石匠们经过无数次试验，终于摸清了红色岩石的特性，找到了对付这种岩石的办法。有了先行者探索的经验，再以师带徒，先后培养出80名合格的石匠，为拱券锻造料石。

渡槽建设的后期，为了加快工程进度，总指挥部又从河顺公社调来250名民工参与施工。庞大的渡槽建设需要大量石料，近处山上能开采的石料都开采过了，后期所需的大量上等石料要从远处的山上开采。从采石场开采出来的石头，必须运到山坡边缘，再从边缘滚下山坡，到达河槽，再从河槽抬到渡槽工地。河顺公社郎垒村的郭世杰在石料场用铁绳捆石头时，在山上向下滚石头的崔书成没注意看下面是否有人，就把一块300多斤重的石头滚了下来。石头从郭世杰右小腿肚边擦过，郭世杰被撞倒在地，疼得直打滚。经医生检查，郭世杰虽然没有骨折，可是却伤得不轻。当时工地上提的口号是"轻伤不下火线"。经简单包扎处理，郭世杰又拄着棍子，忍着疼痛，一瘸一拐地上了工地。大伙劝他休养，他说："我不能干重活，还能干轻活。"可没干多久，腿就疼得像针扎得一样，连站都站不住。领导纷纷劝他回去休息，等养好了伤再继续干。他只好下了工地休养，等伤势稍有好转，就又上了工地。

1961年8月15日，在550人的施工队伍挖掘了5264立方米土石方，垒砌了9318立方米料石后，横跨露水河，长130米，宽11.42米，高11.4米的南谷洞渡槽顺利竣工。

1964年12月，红旗渠总干渠第三期工程竣工。至此，全长70.6公里

Over 50 stonemasons on the site were very familiar with limestone, but it was a tricky problem for them to deal with quartz sandstone which was much harder than limestone. However, the workers did not wait but explored. After numerous trials, the stonemasons finally figured out the characteristics of the red rock and found a way to deal with it. The pioneers gained experience and then taught fresh hands. 80 qualified stonemasons were trained successively to process stones.

In the later stage of the aqueduct construction, in order to speed up the progress of the project, the General Command transferred 250 workers from Heshun Commune to participate in the construction. The huge aqueduct required a large amount of stones, and all the stones in the mountains nearby had already been mined. The fine stones needed in the later period had to be mined from distant mountains. The stones mined from the quarry must be transported to the edge of the hillside, rolled down the hillside to the river channel, and then carried to the aqueduct site. Once, when Guo Shijie from Heshun Commune was tying a stone on the river channel, Cui Shucheng, who was working on the mountain, rolled down a stone weighing more than 150 kilograms without noticing if anyone was below. The stone brushed Guo Shijie's right calf and knocked him down to the ground. He rolled about in pain. The medical examination showed that Guo Shijie was badly hurt although not fractured. At that time, the slogan on the construction site was "Don't leave the front line on account of minor wounds". After a simple medical treatment, Guo Shijie endured the pain and limped to the construction site, leaning on a stick. Everyone advised him to rest, but he said, "I can't do heavy work, but I can do light work." Very soon, his leg was too painful for him to stand. The leaders advised him to go back to rest until he was cured. He had to leave the construction site. When the injury improved slightly, he went to the construction site again.

After the construction team consisting of 550 people carried out 5,264 cubic meters of excavation and 9,318 cubic meters of masonry, the aqueduct named the Nangudong (south valley tunnel) Aqueduct, 130 meters long, 11.42 meters wide and 11.4 meters high, was completed successfully over the Lushuihe River on August 15, 1961.

In December 1964, the third phase of the Hongqiqu General Main Canal was completed. So far, the whole Hongqiqu General Main Canal with a total

1965年4月5日,红旗渠总干渠建成通水
The Hongqiqu General Main Canal came into operation on April 5, 1965

的红旗渠总干渠全线贯通。

1965年4月5日,是中国传统节日——清明节,但这一天对林县人民来说,其意义却不止于此。这天晨星未尽,东方刚露出鱼肚白,总干渠分水岭周边村寨的男女老幼从四面八方向分水岭汇集,来参加在这里举行的红旗渠总干渠通水典礼。

随着闸门提升,红旗渠水奔涌而出,人群沸腾了。千百年来,引漳河水灌溉林县良田的美好愿望终于实现了。这一天虽然等得太久,但欢歌代替了悲叹,开心代替了忧愁,男女老少无不开怀大笑,把心灵深处的快乐毫不吝啬地表达出来。看着这奔流不息的渠水流向林县每一个角落,去拥抱山峦、拥抱村庄、拥抱田野,人们坚信林县从此要鲜活起来了!

length of 70.6 kilometers was completed.

On April 5, 1965, it was a traditional Chinese festival, the Chingming Festival (the Tomb-Sweeping Day), but the significance of this day for the people of Linxian County was far more than that. In the early morning before the sun rose, the local people from the villages around the main canal watershed gathered to participate in the completion ceremony of the Hongqiqu General Main Canal.

As the gates were lifted, the water rushed out and the people were overjoyed. For thousands of years, the wish of diverting the Zhanghe River to irrigate the farmland of Linxian County finally came true. This day was delayed too long, but now the merry songs replaced the lament and the happiness replaced the sorrow. All the people, old and young, laughed and expressed their joy from the bottom of their hearts. Seeing the canal water flowing to every corner of Linxian County to embrace the mountains, the villages and the fields, people firmly believed that Linxian County would have a prosperous future from now on!

三条干渠的修建

伟大的目标在接续奋斗中实现。林县人民并没有因总干渠的通水而沾沾自喜、止步于此，而是不松劲，不停步，再出发，迅速投入林县境内三条干渠的建设中去。

第一干渠自分水岭沿林虑山东侧向南，经水河、黑龙庙、田家沟、黄华、桃园、北小庄、温家掌等村到合涧镇西与英雄渠汇流，全长39.7公里，设计灌溉面积39万亩；第二干渠自分水岭起，经姚村镇东北部猫儿岭，经申家岗、焦家屯、马家山、庞村、皇墓、杨伯山屯、张家井、乔家屯等村，至横水镇马店村东，全长47.6公里，设计灌溉面积14万亩；第三干渠从总干渠尾（分水岭）上游560米处的右侧分出，伸向东北，经仙岩村到下燕科村南穿越卢寨岭曙光洞后，到东卢寨村东，全长10.9公里，设计灌溉面积5万亩。

红旗渠一干渠翻山越岭修到了桃园河边。桃园河是一条季节性河流，虽然只有百余米宽，但岸陡谷深，每到汛期，洪水奔腾咆哮，卧牛般大小的石头也被冲得逐浪翻滚。正当设计人员在这里反复琢磨时，当地老百姓说："这条河又深又陡，平时过河要绕好几里路，到了汛期根本不能通行，闹得两岸是'自古不结亲，隔河不种地'，这次跨河建渡槽，要是通了渠水又能过车走人，那就太好了！"设计人员都感到老百姓的话有道理，可是怎么样才能办到呢?这时路过的一位老人听到设计人员的议论，说道："小水沟上放一根石条，就能经住人走车压，在渡槽上加个盖儿，搞个空心桥，不就既通了水又通了车吗？"老人的话使大家深受启发。是啊！武汉长江大桥不就是既通火车又通汽车吗？咱们

Construction of Three Main Canals

Great goals were achieved in the struggles. The people of Linxian County did not feel complacent or relax because of the completion of the Hongqiqu General Main Canal. Instead, they quickly devoted their energy to the construction of three main canals in Linxian County.

The First Main Canal, with a total length of 39.7 kilometers and a designed irrigation area of 26,000 hectares, flowed south from the east side of the Linlyu Mountain, through the villages of Shuihe, Heilongmiao, Tianjiagou, Huanghua, Taoyuan, Beixiaozhuang, Wenjiazhang, etc. and met the Yingxiong Canal in the west of Hejian Town. The Second Main Canal started from the watershed and ran through Maoerling in the northeast of Yaocun Town, Shenjiagang, Jiaojiatun, Majiashan, Pangcun, Huangmu, Yangboshantun, Zhangjiajing, Qiaojiatun and other villages, and reached the east of Madian Village of Hengshui Town, with a total length of 47.6 kilometers and a designed irrigation area of 9,300 hectares. The Third Main Canal, with a total length of 10.9 kilometers and a designed irrigation area of 3,300 hectares, originated on the right side 560 meters upstream of the end of the General Main Canal, extended to the northeast, passed through Xianyan Village to the south of Xiayanke Village, flowed through the Shuguang Tunnel of the Luzhai Mountain, and reached the east of Dongluzhai Village.

The First Main Canal crossed mountains and arrived at the Taoyuan River. The Taoyuan River was a seasonal river, which was only 100 meters wide with deep and steep valley. In the rainy season, the flood was so violent that huge rocks could be washed downstream. While the designers were pondering over here, the local people said, "The river is deep and steep. Usually, we need to cross the river by a circuitous route of several miles, but it's impassable in flood season. Therefore, 'no cross river marriage, no cross river farming'. If the aqueduct to be built here across the river is passable for both water and traffic, it would be great!" The designers felt that the local resident's words made sense, but how could they achieve it? An old man passing by heard the designers' argument and said, "If you put a stone plate on a ditch, it will withstand the pressure of traffic. If you put a cover on the aqueduct to make a hollow bridge, it will be passable for both water and traffic!" The old man's words inspired everyone. Yes! Both trains and cars were

这个渡槽就不能既通水又通车吗？大家的思路一下子打通了：把渡槽与渡桥合二为一进行设计！

这样的设计好倒是好，可是渠水带来的泥沙淤积的问题又该如何解决呢？平时渠水会携带一定的泥沙，汛期更甚。如果听任泥沙淤积，天长日久，势必会造成渠道堵塞。在明渠上清淤并不是什么难事，现在要把渡槽变渡桥，明渠变成了暗渠，清淤就成了大问题。希望很快变成了失望，又如何在这失望中寻找新的希望呢？时间一天天地在设计人员的冥思苦想中流逝。一天，突然有人说，不管是自然河流，还是人工渠道，凡是水流湍急的地方都没有泥沙沉积现象，这是为什么呢？大伙儿一听都兴奋起来了，立即进行了试验，发现水的流速越大，水中携带的泥沙越不容易沉积。如果把渡槽的落差加大，以此提高水的流速，泥沙就无法沉积，问题不就解决了吗？

泥沙淤积的问题解决了，桥墩的承受力的问题又暴露出来了。渡槽与渡桥合二为一，必然加大对桥墩的压力。这件事看起来并不难，只要把桥墩砌得粗大些就行了。但是，这在平常看来很简单的问题，在这里却行不通，因为渡桥桥墩不仅要承受渡桥的压力，还要承受汛期洪水的巨大冲击力。从承压能力方面说，桥墩越粗大，承压能力越强。而从抗洪水的冲击力看，桥墩越粗大，受的洪水的冲击力也越大。加粗加大桥墩，会使洪水的排泄受阻，使得洪水对桥墩的冲击力增强，反而增加了桥墩受冲击的风险。这样一来，桥墩既要承受来自纵向的压力，又要抵御来自底部洪水的横向冲击力，哪一个都不能削弱，怎样解决这个矛盾呢？设计人员通过反复考虑，终于找到了一个解决这个两难问题的办法：变桥墩的迎水面为迎水线，就是把桥墩迎水面的椭圆形建成三角

passable on the Wuhan Yangtze River Bridge! Could the aqueduct be designed to be accessible to both water and traffic? A good idea was born: the aqueduct and the bridge could be designed as one!

The design scheme was perfect, but how did one solve the problem of sedimentation caused by the canal water? Usually, the water would carry a certain amount of sediment, and this situation would be more serious in the flood season. If the sediment was accumulated for a long time, it was bound to cause blockage in the canal. It was not difficult to dredge in an open canal. Now the aqueduct was to be turned into a bridge and the open canal into a culvert, and dredging became a big problem. Hope soon became disappointment. How could they find new hope in this disappointment? The designers worked hard each day as time was rapidly passing. One day, somebody suddenly said that no matter whether it was a natural river or a man-made canal, there was no sediment deposition where the current was rushing. Why? As soon as they heard this, people were excited and immediately carried out the experiment and found that the greater the flow rate of water, the less easily the sediment carried in the water would deposit. If the slope in the aqueduct was increased to speed up the velocity of the water, the sediment would not be deposited, and the problem would be solved, wouldn't it?

The problem of sedimentation deposition was solved, and the problem of the bearing capacity of the piers was exposed. The aqueduct and the bridge were combined into one, which inevitably increased the pressure on the piers. This problem did not seem to be difficult to solve as long as the thickness of the piers was increased. However, this solution did not work here because the piers were subject to not only the pressure of the bridge, but also the huge impact of the flood in the flood season. From the perspective of pressure bearing capacity, the thicker the piers, the stronger the pressure bearing capacity. In terms of the impact of the flood, the thicker the piers, the greater the impact of the flood on the piers. Thick piers would affect the smooth discharge of the flood, which would strengthen the flood impact on the piers and increase the risk of damage. In this way, the piers had to bear both longitudinal pressure from the culvert bridge and lateral impact force from the flood, neither of which could be weakened. How to solve this contradiction? After repeated consideration, the designers finally found a solution to this dilemma, i.e., to change the upstream face of the piers,

形。这样在不减少桥墩承压力的同时，大大减少了洪水对桥墩的冲击力，圆满完成了整个渡桥的设计任务。

设计中的问题一个接一个地被解决了，施工中的难题又一个接一个地出现了。建设这样一座100米长、24米高，由7个桥孔组成的大渡桥，大量的工作是砌桥墩、拱桥券。按常规，施工的方法是用大量的木料搭脚手架和拱架，这样至少需要上好的木料3000根。可这时红旗渠全线都在施工，到处都需要木料，总指挥部只能提供1000根左右的木料，必须想个节省木料的好办法。林县人民从长期的劳动实践中受到了启发。民工们想到了自己家盖房子，谁用过脚手架？都是蹲在墙上头垒墙的，既然在家盖房垒墙时这个方法可行，在建桥墩时为啥就不能蹲在桥墩上垒砌呢？有位老石匠说："在修总干渠的时候，咱们在悬崖峭壁上砌四五米高的渠墙，不也没有搭过脚手架吗？还不都是蹲在渠墙上垒的？垒桥墩也不用搭架了，这样既省时间还省木料。"大家纷纷出主意想办法，经过认真论证后，指挥部最终采取了不搭脚手架的方案。施工时，让在高处砌桥墩的民工身上系上安全绳，这样既保证了施工人员的安全，又使工程能够正常进行。

搭脚手架的木料省下来了，但架拱券仍需要搭拱架。按惯例，搭拱架需要从地面开始。这个渡桥高、孔眼大，而且承受力又大，要经得起几十吨的重压，搭这样的拱架还是需要大量的木料，可现实问题是木料严重不足，这个任务几乎是不可能完成的。要把这种不可能变为可能，只能靠发挥建设者的聪明才智了。经过多次测算，设计者决定不在地面开始搭拱架，而是在桥墩20米高处开始搭拱架。他们先把一根横木

turning the oval shape of the piers into a triangle. In this way, without reducing the bearing pressure of the piers, the impact of the flood on the piers was greatly reduced, and the design task of the entire culvert bridge was successfully completed.

The problems in the design were solved one by one, and the problems in the construction appeared one after another. To construct such a 100-meter-long and 24-meter-high culvert bridge consisting of 7 bridge holes, the main work was to build piers and arches. As usual, the method of construction was to build scaffolding and arch support with a large amount of wood, so that at least 3,000 pieces of good wood were needed. Meanwhile, the entire project of the Hongqiqu Canal was under construction. Wood was needed everywhere. The General Command could only provide about 1,000 pieces of wood. It was necessary to think of a good way to save wood. The people of Linxian County were inspired by long-term labor practices. The workers thought of building houses in their own homes. No one had used scaffolding. People were squatting on the top of the wall to build the wall. Since this method could get into effect to build walls in their homes, why not squat on the pier to build the piers? An old stonemason said, "In the construction of the General Main Canal, we built four-to-five-meter-high canal walls on the cliffs without scaffolding. We were all squatting on the canal wall to work. So, we don't need scaffolding to build the piers. It saves time and wood." Everyone was trying to come up with ideas. After careful argumentations, a plan without scaffolding was finally adopted. Safety ropes were attached to the workers who worked on the piers high above ground, which ensured the safety of the construction workers and enabled the works to proceed normally.

The timber for scaffolding had been saved, but building arches still needed arch support. Traditionally, the arch support needed to be built from the ground. This culvert bridge was very high with large openings and the huge bearing capacity needed to withstand dozens of tons of pressure. It still required a lot of wood to erect such arch supports, but the problem was that there was a serious shortage of wood, and this task was almost impossible to complete. Only the builders' wisdom could make this impossible task possible. After many calculations, the designers decided not to erect the arch supports on the ground, but at the height of 20 meters of the piers. They first put a horizontal wood

架在两个桥墩之间,以此为基础面开始往上搭,这样就可以省下地面至起架处的木料。可是待到起架时,又出现了一个新问题:两个桥墩相距8米,这样长的木料根本找不到,又无法搭架。木料不够长,怎样才能让它"长"起来呢?农民技术员路银想了个土办法:在两个桥墩上砌上几对又厚又长的石条,从桥墩向外伸出0.6米,这样两个桥墩就相对拉近了1米多,木料不就"长"了1米多吗?这样,桥墩就像巨人伸出的大"手",稳稳地架住了放在上面的木料,既不影响起架,也不影响桥墩的垒砌,人们把这种架桥法称为"简易拱桥法"。

自1965年9月1日开工到1966年4月5日,一座上面走汽车、中间走渠水、下面走洪水的三用渡桥——桃园河渡桥顺利竣工。该工程共挖土石方5400立方米,砌石5600立方米,投工6万个,投资5.4万元。

古希腊人阿基米德说:"给我一个支点,我可以撬起整个地球。"但他终其一生也没找到这个支点。而河顺分指挥部要建的二干渠上的夺丰渡槽,却有一个支点。这座长413米,最高处14米,宽5米,过水流量2.7立方米/秒,50个跨径5米的桥孔构成的渡槽,在其上半部有一座小山作支点,把渡槽分为上下两段:上段长172米,17个拱孔;下段长241米,33个拱孔,一山担两边,支撑着渡槽。

整座渡槽建设共砌石2.15万立方米,但在这里不是所有的石头都能用来建设渡槽的。必须根据石头的性状、肌理、强度、储量以及可开采性等因素来选择。要在工地周边找到能够开采2万多立方米的优质石材的采石场并非易事。负责开采石料的民工在附近的山上打开了一处又一

between two piers and then set up the arch supports on the wooden base. By this way, the wood materials from the ground to that wooden base could be saved. However, there arose a new problem. The two piers were eight meters apart, and it was impossible to find such a long timber. The wood was not long enough, how could we make it "longer"? The farmer technician Lu Yin thought of an indigenous method: several pairs of thick and long stone slabs were laid on the two piers, extending 0.6 meters outward from the piers, so that the two piers were more than one meter closer to each other. Then, wasn't the timber more than one meter "longer"? In this way, the piers were like a giant's huge "hands" which steadily held the timber placed on them. It neither affected the erecting of the arch support, nor the construction of the piers. People called this method the "simple arch method".

Starting on September 1, 1965, the culvert bridge of the Taoyuan River was successfully completed on April 5, 1966. It was a three-purpose culvert bridge, with the top layer for cars, the next layer for canal water and the openings below for flood water. For this project, 5,400 cubic meters of excavation and 5,600 cubic meters of masonry were completed, with 60,000 man-days and a cost of 54,000 yuan.

The ancient Greek Archimedes said, "Give me a pivot, I can prize up the earth." But he never found this pivot all his life. However, there was a pivot in the Duofeng Aqueduct to be built by the Heshun Branch Command. The aqueduct was 413 meters long, 14 meters high and 5 meters wide, with a water flow of 2.7 cubic meters per second and 50 bridge holes with a diameter of 5 meters. The aqueduct was supported by a hill, which divided the aqueduct into two sections: the upstream section was 172 meters long with 17 arch holes and the downstream section was 241 meters long with 33 arch holes. A mountain supported the aqueduct on both sides.

A total of 21,500 cubic meters of masonry was built for the aqueduct, but not all stones could be used to build aqueducts. Stones must be chosen according to factors such as traits, texture, strength, reserve volume and exploitability. It was not easy to find a quarry that could provide more than 20,000 cubic meters of high-quality stones around the construction site. The workers responsible for mining stones excavated one place after another in the nearby mountains. Either

处，不是石质不好就是储量不够。优中选优就不可避免地要舍近求远。最终人们在距离施工地2.5公里外的地方找到了适合的采石场。

开采石灰岩性质的料石不像劈山开路或凿洞，不能用烈性黄色炸药狂炸滥崩，那样的话只会炸出一堆石碴，不仅无法整理成适用的料石，还会破坏石材内部的肌理，降低石材的强度。开采量小的话，主要靠人工用钢钎和铁撬杠将石料撬开。要是开采量大，仅靠人工用撬杠撬耗时费力，这时就需要用威力较小的黑色炸药炸松。用黑色炸药炸松巨大的石块后，仍然要靠人力将其分解成能够搬运的小块儿。这样的石头只是荒石（原石），还需要锻造成料石。一般来说，在采石场就地把荒石锻造成料石，可以减少运输工作量。但在长途搬运过程中难免出现磕碰，会损坏料石的边角，料石的质量无法得到保证。因此渡槽的建设者们宁可在运输上多费力气，也不让料石受损，就改石场锻料为工地锻料。

根据测算，要把近3万立方米的石材从2.5公里外的地方运到渡槽工地，需要3个月时间。运输所占用的时间比砌筑用的时间还长。为了提高运输效率，河顺公社把运输任务分解到各村。各村把群众动员起来，男女老少齐上阵，大车小车齐出动，马车、牛车拉，独轮车推，肩膀扛，牲口驮，连孩子们放学也要捎块石头到工地上，运送石材的路上车水马龙，这样只用了不到一个月的时间就完成了全部的运料任务。

石头运回来了，剩下的就该石匠们大显身手了。石料选材上，厚度不能小于20厘米，宽度不少于30厘米。加工时要达到上、下、左、右、

the quality was poor or the reserves were not enough. If you want to choose the best materials, you would inevitably have to go far. Later, people found a suitable quarry in a place 2.5 kilometers away from the construction site.

Mining limestone materials was not like splitting a mountain to open a road or digging a tunnel. High explosive could not be used, otherwise, only a pile of ballast would be mined, which would not only fail to produce suitable stones, but also destroy the internal texture and reduce the strength. If the amount of mining was small, the stones were mainly pried open manually with steel chisels and iron crowbars. If the amount of mining was large, it was time-consuming and laborious to pry manually, so stones needed to be loosened with less powerful black explosives. After blowing up the huge stones with black explosives, it was still necessary to break them down into small pieces that could be carried. Such stones were just raw stones, which needed to be processed into stone blocks. Generally speaking, processing raw stones into stone blocks in the quarry could reduce the transportation workload. However, collisions would inevitably occur during long-distance transportation, which would damage the edges and corners of the stones, and the quality of the stones could not be guaranteed. Therefore, the builders of the aqueduct would rather put more effort into transportation than damage the stones. The stones were processed on the construction site rather than in the quarry.

According to calculations, it would take three months to transport nearly 30,000 cubic meters of stones from the quarry 2.5 kilometers away to the aqueduct site. The time for transportation would be longer than the time for building masonry. In order to improve transportation efficiency, Heshun Commune divided the transportation tasks among the villages, which mobilized all the villagers, men and women, old and young, and all the means of transportation, cattle carts and unicycles, or on shoulders and animals. Even the children would take stones to the construction site after school. In this way, it took only less than a month to complete all the transportation tasks.

The stones were transported to the site, and it was time for the stonemasons to show their skills. The stone to be processed should be no less than 20 centimeters thick and 30 centimeters wide. It shall be processed into a block with five flat surfaces, top, bottom, left, right and front, and with four sides vertical.

前五面平整，四边垂直。料石表面1分米的宽度内用錾凿出三道纹路，几乎是一道挨一道。渡槽是按层砌筑的，必须统一厚度，石料加工好后，将厚度写在料石上，分类堆放。要保证砌体的完整性，还需要大量较长的石料作钉石，其小面为主面，分别加工，分别堆存，便于取用。

料石备齐，砌筑开始。每一层都是砌几块方石，就砌一块钉石。钉石就像钉子一样，长长的身躯钉入砌体深处，把砌体联结成整体。每一个桥墩的迎水面和背水面都砌成立体三角形，组成这种立体三角形的砌石就叫墩面石。墩面自下而上逐渐收小，形体不断变化，形成一定的坡面。一块墩面石一个尺寸，不得有丝毫差错。这样的难度，施工者不可贸然垒砌，需要用纸板做出模型，然后根据样板砌筑。

渡槽砌筑到设计的高度时，就开始起拱。拱券石分拱脸石和内拱石两种。在拱券体前、后两个表面外露的由一块块拱石砌成的扇形拱口叫拱脸石，前后拱脸石之间的拱石叫内拱石。拱券能否凳成，关键在拱脸石。拱脸石统领内拱石，把拱脸石凳成功了，内拱石依次垒砌就容易了。拱脸石皆为单数，加工拱脸石之前，要根据拱弧的半径、拱弧的弧度和所能提供的石块的尺寸，将拱弧平分成单数的若干小段，再减去所有灰缝占去的长度，剩下的就是每一块拱脸石的尺寸，据此对拱脸石进行锻造。弧形的拱券决定了拱脸石要加工成梯形，大面在上，小面在下，这就必须严格掌握尺寸，稍有差池拱券就不能合拢。如果说墙面石要求五个面保证平整，那么，拱脸石则要求六个面都要平整，而且还要

Three lines shall be chiseled every one decimeter wide, almost one line next to another. The aqueduct was built layer by layer, and the thickness must be equal. After being processed, the stone was marked with its thickness and stacked in categories. In order to ensure the integrity of the masonry, a large number of long stone materials were required as nail stones, with the small end as main surface, and they were processed and stored separately for easy access.

After the stones were ready, the masonry work started. In each layer, one nail stone was placed every several square stones. The nail stone was like a nail hammered into the depth of the masonry, connecting the masonry into a whole. The upstream surface and the downstream surface of each pier were built into a triangle, and the stones forming the triangle were called pier facing stones. The pier surface gradually decreased from bottom to top, and its shape changed constantly, forming a certain slope. Each pier facing stone had a specific size and the workers could not make any mistakes. It was so difficult that the constructors could not build it as usual, and it was necessary to make a cardboard model and then build it according to the model.

When the aqueduct was built to the designed height, the arch began to be built. The arch stones were divided into two types: arch face stones and inner arch stones. The arch stones exposed upstream and downstream and forming the fan-shaped arch openings were called arch face stones. The arch stones between the upstream and downstream arch face stones were called inner arch stones. Whether the arch could be formed, the key process lied in the arch face stones. The arch face stones dominated the inner arch stone. Once the arch face stones were successfully placed, it would be easy to place the inner arch stones in turn. The quantity of arch face stones was of odd number. Before the arch face stones were processed, according to the radius of the arch and the size of the stones to be used, the arch was divided equally into several segments, the size of which could be calculated with the width of joints subtracted, and then the arch face stones were processed accordingly. The curved arch determined that the arch face stones should be processed into a trapezoidal shape with the large side up and the small side down. Thus, the size must be strictly controlled, and the arch could not be formed even with the slightest mistake. If the stones of wall surface required five faces to be flat, then the arch face stones required six faces to be flat and polished

反复打磨。拱脸石之所以分成单数,除了外观上的美观外,为的是最后一块拱脸石正好在拱顶处合拢。这块用于封顶的单数的拱脸石,其长度和厚度要稍大于其他拱脸石,防止撤除拱胎时拱顶下沉。所有拱脸石加工完毕后,先逐块在空地上试砌,不符合拱券设计形状的,要就地修整,直到合乎要求,以最大限度减少垒砌拱券时因加工不到位引发的窝工。

渡槽上每一块石头都有自己的位置,相互依存,都有着不可替代的作用。拱座石承担全部石拱的轴向压力和水平推力,尺寸一般要大一些。180°的拱弧拱座石是水平的,直接在上面砌拱石。拱券以上紧贴圆弧部分的料石为护拱石,其一端要与拱券外弧吻合,圆弧坡度由低到高不断变化,护拱石的咬合面的斜度也要随之变化,才能永远保持吻合。

来自地下的2万多立方米粗糙且没有生命的石头,经工匠们巧夺天工的手把它们砌在一起,相互支撑,相互咬合,凝结成一个生命共同体,成为具有实用价值的艺术精品。3100名民工苦干125天,砌石料1.02万立方米,投工21.5万个,投资12万元,最终于1966年4月5日建成了这座寓意人寿年丰的夺丰渡槽。

我们知道,两点之间直线距离最短,在修筑道路和渠道时,当遭遇高山峻岭的阻挡,为缩短距离,经常要挖掘隧洞穿越。一般情况下隧洞中心线无疑应布置成直线,这样洞线最短,工程量最小,便于测量放线

壮观的夺丰渡槽
The spectacular Duofeng Aqueduct

repeatedly. The reason why the quantity of arch face stones was of odd number, in addition to the aesthetic appearance, was that the last arch face stone was placed at the vault. The last stone used for capping was slightly longer and thicker than other arch face stones in order to prevent the vault from descending when the arch support was removed. After all the arch face stones were processed, the workers would experiment with the laying of arch face stones one by one on the ground. Any stones that did not match the designed shape would be trimmed on site until they met the requirements, so as to minimize the time loss caused by inaccurate stone processing.

Every stone on the aqueduct had its own position, which was interdependent and had an irreplaceable role. The arch base stones undertook the axial pressure and the horizontal thrust of the whole arch, and its size was generally larger. The arch base stone was horizontal and arch stones were laid directly on it. The stone above the arch was a guard stone, one end of which should be matched with the outer arc of the arch. The slope of the arc changed continuously from low to high, and the inclination of the guard stone's end should also change accordingly so as to maintain the combined condition forever.

Through the magical hands of artisans, more than 20,000 cubic meters of rough and inanimate stones were built together, supported each other, formed a community of life, and became a fine work of art with practical value. After working hard for 125 days, 3,100 workers built 10,200 cubic meters of masonry. With 215,000 man-days and a cost of 120,000 yuan, the Duofeng Aqueduct was completed on April 5, 1966, which symbolized longevity and prosperity.

The straight-line distance between two points is the shortest. When people built roads and channels and encountered the obstacles of high mountains, tunnels are often excavated in order to shorten the distance. Generally, there was no doubt that the centerline of the tunnel should be arranged in a straight line, so that the tunnel line was the shortest, the work quantity was the smallest, it

和开挖时掌握方向，施工比较容易。然而，红旗渠三干渠上的曙光洞却似乎违背了常识，4千米长的隧洞不是直线而是折线，这其中隐藏着什么样的奥秘呢？曙光洞要穿越的芦寨岭是由火石山、豹子山、芦寨岭三座山岭构成的，因芦寨岭最高，统称芦寨岭。作为红旗渠上洞线最长的隧洞，必须开挖竖井来增加工作面和通风、出渣。曙光洞施工若采取直线掘进，多数竖井将位于高山顶上，竖井挖得过深，工程量过大，掘进和出渣都很困难，施工时间也要延长。要使竖井的定位与地形相匹配，从而减少工程量，又要使隧洞能顺利贯通，这对工程建设者来说是一个巨大的挑战。建设者们以非常之策略干非常之事，应对挑战的方法就是"力争竖井线，隧洞呈折线"，在定线时放弃直线掘进，根据地形起伏情况，避高就低，将洞线沿地势低处布置，成为多折线的隧洞。如此这般，虽然洞线长了，竖井多了，但工作面增加了，施工难度降低了，大大加快了工程进度。

1964年11月17日，曙光洞放响了开工的第一炮。东岗公社一个村包打一个竖井，13000名男女，肩负着几代人对水的期盼，认准目标，

开凿曙光洞
Excavating the Shuguang Tunnel

was convenient to survey and master the direction during excavation, and the construction could be easier for workers. However, the Shuguang Tunnel on the Hongqiqu Third Main Canal seemed to be contrary to common sense. The 4-kilometer-long tunnel was not in a straight line but a polyline. What kind of mystery was hidden in it? The Luzhai Mountain, which the Shuguang Tunnel would cross, was composed of the Huoshi Mountain, the Baozi Mountain and the Luzhai Mountain. Because Luzhai Mountain was the highest among them, they were collectively known as Luzhai Mountain. As the longest tunnel on the Hongqiqu Canal, shafts must be excavated to increase working surfaces, ventilation and mucking. If the Shuguang Tunnel was excavated in a straight line, most of the shafts would be located on the top of the mountain. The shafts would be too deep with an extremely large amount of work, so that the excavation and mucking would be very difficult, and the construction period would also be prolonged. It was a huge challenge for the project builders to match the positioning of the shafts with the terrain, thereby reducing the amount of work, and complete the tunnel smoothly. The builders did extraordinary things with extraordinary tactics, and the way to deal with the challenge was "Priority to the shaft line to leave the tunnel a polyline". During the setting-out, the straight-line was given up and the polyline was adopted to locate the tunnel in low areas according to the topographic fluctuation. In this way, although the tunnel line was longer with more shafts, the working surfaces were increased and the construction difficulty was reduced, thereby greatly accelerating the progress of the project.

On November 17, 1964, the Shuguang Tunnel carried out the first blasting of the construction. In Donggang Commune, each village undertook the task of digging one shaft. 13,000 men and women of the commune shouldered several

高歌猛进，依靠团队，锲而不舍。万余人的队伍分布在隧洞的出入口和34个竖井工地上，没有升降机，没有大型水泵，没有鼓风机，没有电器照明，没有传送带出渣，民工们硬是凭着一身的力气和不服输的精神与天斗，与地斗，与各种困难斗。竖井出渣需要提升工具，他们自制了直径超大的辘轳和绞磨。辘轳一次提升120~150公斤土渣，绞磨一次提升150~200公斤土渣，较深的竖井多用绞磨。出渣和井下作业不能同时进行，向上提渣时，井下的人要紧贴井壁，筐不能装得太满，以免落石伤人。平洞出渣所需的运载工具抬筐、小推车、架子车、斗车都是人们自己从家带。出渣时，距离近的就人工挑抬，直接装筐运出洞外；距离远的，就改用小推车、架子车或斗车装运。没有电器照明的条件，他们利用大块的玻璃镜反射太阳光线进入洞内，再辅之以马灯进行照明。阴天和夜间借不上阳光，只好加大马灯数量。没有鼓风机，洞内通风不畅，人们就把村里碾米用的扇车搬到工地，靠手摇扇车向洞内送风。送风需风管，没有风管人们就用帆布袋代替。爆破后洞内会产生大量硝烟，靠自然排烟每次需4个小时以上。为了不耽误时间，竖井排烟就在筐上绑上树枝，用辘轳一遍一遍地上下提升加快排烟；在平洞内先用土风车鼓风，然后人们进洞挥动衣服，里外来回跑动往外赶烟。没有深井水泵，在20米深的竖井里就采用小型水泵接力排水，即在井壁的腰间开一个小型旁洞放置汽油桶，下一级将水抽到桶里，上一级再把桶里的水抽出井外。

generations' expectations for water. They focused on the goal with perseverance and supported each other as a team. The team of more than 10,000 people was distributed in the entrance and exit of the tunnel and on 34 shaft construction sites. There were no lifts, large pumps, blowers, electrical lighting or conveyor belts, but workers relied on the spirit of not admitting defeat and physical strength to fight against all kinds of difficulties. The excavated material of the shaft required lifting tools, and they made windlasses and winches with large diameter. The windlass could lift 120~150 kilograms of excavated material at a time, and the winch 150~200 kilograms, which was often used for deeper shafts. Lifting excavated material and downhole operations could not be carried out at the same time. When lifting excavated material upwards, the workers in the shaft should stand closely to the well wall, and the baskets should not be filled too much in order to prevent falling rocks from hurting workers. The tools required for mucking in the tunnel, such as baskets, carts, trolleys and bucket carts were all brought from local people's homes. If it was close to the portal, the workers would carry excavated material out of the tunnel by man power. If it was far, small carts and trolleys would be used. Without electrical lights, they used large glass mirrors to reflect the sun's rays into the tunnel, supplemented by kerosene lanterns. There was no sunlight on cloudy days and at night, they had to use more kerosene lanterns. Without blowers, the tunnel was not well ventilated, and the villagers brought the fans for rice milling to the construction site to blow the wind into the tunnel. Without air pipes, they used canvas bags instead to send air. After blasting, a large amount of smoke would be generated in the tunnel. It took more than four hours for the smoke to dissipate naturally every time. In order to save the construction time, for the ventilation in the shaft, tree branches were tied to the basket, and the windlass was used to lift it up and down again and again to speed up the ventilation. For the ventilation in the tunnel, the blowers made by the workers were used to send fresh air into the tunnel first, and then people ran back and forth in the tunnel, waving their clothes to drive the smoke out. Without deep-well pumps, they drained the water in the 20-meter-deep shaft by relay pumping with small water pumps, i.e., a hole was excavated in the middle of the well wall to place a gasoline barrel. Water was pumped from the shaft bottom into the barrel, and then pumped out of the shaft.

工地上的日子像太阳绞着的辘轳一样，缓慢而沉重地轮回。竖井的开挖主要靠炸药，先在竖井的正中心掏一个深1米、直径0.3米、装药6公斤的炮眼进行爆破，再用小炮把四周剩下的岩石进行爆破，使竖井达到设计要求。每24小时爆破一次，日均进度0.5米。为了兼顾井下施工，每天分为4班，每班6个小时，每井每班7人，井下5人施工，井上2人绞辘轳送人上下井和提升出渣。井深超过20米的，井上加到4人。前两班主要是打炮眼、装药、放炮，后两班负责放小炮、修边和出渣。对于有地下水的竖井，就采取小炮群，边打炮眼边排水。炮眼深不超过1米，装药量是眼深的一半，最多不超过三分之二。炸药要用塑料纸包装，避免受潮阻爆。出水量较大、水位较深的竖井，则采用电雷管引爆。

这种日复一日的上下井和爆破作业，几乎每天都在与死神博弈。下燕科大队的大队长张家俊，十几岁时就参了军，并在部队入了党。退役回到村里后，他当上了村干部。打曙光洞时，他们村包打的是18号竖井，张家俊任"井长"。他每天都是第一个下竖井，待他查看没有什么危险之后，再招呼别人下井。出事那天的早上，也许冥冥中有什么预感，他拿着党费登记本向党支部交了党费，然后赶往工地。他又是第一个下井，当下到半中间时，大绳突然断开，接着保护绳也断了，他的身体在下坠过程中不住地在井壁上来回碰撞，最后跌进了深深的洞底。当人们找到他时，他的身体都散架了，遗体是用筐子兜上来的，他年仅38岁。

The daily life on the construction site was repeated again and again with heavy and long-time work. The excavation of the shaft mainly relied on explosives. First, a blast hole with a depth of one meter and a diameter of 0.3 meter was excavated and then charged with 6 kilograms of explosives for a blasting, and then the remaining rock was removed with small blastings to make the shaft meet the design requirements. Blasting was carried out once every 24 hours, with a construction progress of 0.5 meter per day. In order to balance the underground construction, a day was divided into four shifts, with 6 hours a shift. With 7 people per shift per shaft, 5 people were arranged to work in the shaft and two people on the ground operated the windlass to transport people and excavated material. If the depth of the shaft exceeded 20 meters, people on the ground were increased to four. The first two shifts were mainly responsible for drilling, charging, and blasting. The following two shifts were responsible for small blasting, trimming and mucking. For shafts with underground water, small blastings were carried out. Drilling and drainage proceeded together. The depth of the blast holes was no more than one meter, and the charge of explosives was half of the depth and no more than two-thirds. Explosives should be packed in plastic paper to prevent moisture. In shafts with a large amount of water or deep water, blasting was triggered with electric detonators.

Working in the shaft and blasting were like playing against the god of death every day. Zhang Jiajun, the leader of the Xiayanke team, joined the army when he was a teenager and joined the Communist Party of China in the army. After retiring to the village, he became a village leader. During the construction of the Shuguang Tunnel, Zhang Jiajun's village was in charge of the No. 18 shaft and Zhang Jiajun was nominated as the "shaft leader". He was the first person to go down the shaft every day. After he was sure that there was no danger, he informed others to go down. On the morning of the accident, he had a vague premonition. After handing over the Party fees to the Party branch, he rushed to the construction site. He was the first to go down the shaft again. When he was halfway down, the main rope suddenly broke, and then the protective rope was broken too. He began falling, colliding back and forth on the shaft wall, and finally fell to the bottom. When people found him, his body was smashed and had to be carried out of the shaft in a basket. He was only 38 years old.

9号竖井由罗匡村负责，罗匡村的退伍军人王金喜担任"井长"。1965年9月30日下午，按照常规，收工前照例先放炮，然后吃晚饭，饭后紧接着连夜出渣。"井长"金喜与王庭栋、王书林、王四马4个年轻人匆匆吃了晚饭就赶到9号井下，查看爆炸情况。在黑暗的井内，他们提着马灯仔细地一处一处查看，发现了一个哑炮。按规定，为安全起见，哑炮是不允许掏的。可是如果不掏的话，这个在坚硬的岩层上花费2天时间辛辛苦苦打成的炮眼就白白浪费了，而且对下一步的出渣也会留下安全隐患。他们四人决定把这个哑炮的炸药掏出来再重新装填，让它爆炸把岩石崩下来，同时也消除了隐患。在昏暗的灯光下，他们一点一点地小心抠着炮眼封口的泥巴。差不多已经抠完了，就在大家停下来，准备喘口气的时候，"轰"地一声，哑炮炸了，四个人全都倒在了血泊当中，失去了知觉。闻声而来的人们把四个血肉模糊的人升上井去，送到公社卫生院。经抢救，王金喜左手从手腕处被炸断、右眼失明；王庭栋右眼眼球摘除；王书林眼角炸开一道血口；王四马双目失明。他们四人中，王书林、王庭栋30岁，王金喜、王四马才20多岁。

　　曙光洞地质情况复杂，土夹石的流沙层、极为破碎的岩石断层、裂隙出水层交替出现。26号竖井底部的平洞打到100米时，发生了严重塌方。东芦寨连长王师存和民工付黑旦被塌方堵在了洞里。生死关头，他们相互鼓励，拼命用工具从里向外挖了一条生命通道。挖着挖着，空气渐渐稀薄了，马灯灭了，呼吸也不顺畅了，他们只好停下来保持体力。他俩都知道这意味着什么，付黑旦说："我们今天要死在这儿了。"王师存说："外边的人肯定会营救我们。"在死一样的沉寂中，王师存用钢钎猛击洞壁，向外传递消息。外边的人听到里边传来的敲击声，全力抢救，最终从塌方顶部挖了个豁口，把他俩人救了出去。在黑暗中诞生

The No. 9 shaft was under the responsibility of Luokuang Village, with Wang Jinxi, a veteran, as the "shaft leader". On the afternoon of September 30, 1965, the blasting was carried out as usual before the dinner was served, and the mucking would be completed overnight after the meal. Wang Jinxi, Wang Tingdong, Wang Shulin and Wang Sima ate dinner hurriedly and rushed into the No. 9 shaft to check the explosion. In the dark shaft, they looked over carefully with lamps and found a dumb blasting. According to the regulations, the dumb blast hole was not allowed to be touched for safety's sake. But if it was not cleared, the blast hole that was drilled for two days on the hard rock would be wasted, and leave a great risk to the following mucking. They decided to take out the explosives of this dumb blast hole and refill it, so as to blow up the rock and eliminate the hidden danger. In the dim light, they removed the covering mud carefully little by little. They almost finished it and stopped to catch their breath. Just then, the dumb blast hole exploded. The four people fell unconscious in a pool of blood. Hearing the explosion, people rushed to the shaft, lifted the four wounded people out of the shaft and sent them to the commune's health center. Wang Jinxi's left hand was blown up from the wrist and the right eye was blind. Wang Tingdong's right eyeball had to be removed. Wang Shulin's eye corner was wounded. Wang Sima's eyes were blind. Among them, Wang Shulin and Wang Tingdong were both 30 years old while Wang Jinxi and Wang Sima were only in their twenties.

The Shuguang Tunnel had complex geological conditions, such as shifting sand layer, extremely broken rock fault and fissure water emergence layer. When the tunnel at the bottom of the No. 26 shaft reached 100 meters, a serious collapse occurred. Wang Shicun, the team leader of Dongluzhai Village, and Fu Heidan, a worker, were blocked in the tunnel by the collapse. At the moment of life and death, they encouraged each other and worked hard to dig a life channel from the inside out. After digging for a while, the air was getting thinner, the lantern was gone, the breathing was not smooth, and they had to stop to maintain their strength. Both of them knew what it meant, and Fu Heidan said, "We are going to die here today." But Wang Shicun said, "The people outside will definitely rescue us." In the silence of death, Wang Shicun knocked the wall with steel brazing to send a message to the outside . The workers outside heard the knocking sound and rescued them. The Shuguang Tunnel, a four-kilometer tunnel born in

的4公里渠道，曙光洞，在1966年4月5日全线竣工。

1966年4月15日，总长101.5公里的红旗渠三条干渠全部竣工，比原定5月1日的竣工时间提前了15天。三条干渠如三条巨龙，盘绕在林县的山地丘陵间。1966年4月20日，中共林县县委举行红旗渠三条干渠竣工通水庆祝大会，一干渠与英雄渠水汇合而来，翻起一道道雪白的浪花；二干渠渠水流过夺丰渡槽越过林县边界直达安阳县的长虹渡槽；三干渠的水流穿过曙光洞，奔向了迎接它的人群。渠岸上一位老人用绳子系着茶缸，从渠里舀一杯水饮下，这是他平生第一次喝到漳河水。渠道沿线的群众纷纷跑上渠岸，跟着水流奔跑。群山含笑，万众欢腾。所有吃过的苦，都变成了绵延不绝的渠岸，所有流的汗，都化作了奔腾的渠水，所有的付出和牺牲不就为了这一天吗？

红旗渠三条干渠通水典礼主会场

The main venue for the completion ceremony of the three main canals of the Hongqiqu Canal

darkness, was completed on April 5, 1966.

On April 15, 1966, three main canals of the Hongqiqu Canal with a total length of 101.5 kilometers were completed 15 days earlier than the scheduled completion date of May 1. The three main canals went around the mountains and hills in Linxian County. On April 20, 1966, the Linxian County Committee held a celebration meeting for the completion of the three main canals. The First Main Canal and the Yingxiong Canal merged, turning up snow-white waves. The Second Main Canal water flowed through the Duofeng Aqueduct and Linxian County to the Changhong Aqueduct in Anyang County. The water from the Third Main Canal passed through the Shuguang Tunnel and rushed to the people who were welcoming it. On the bank of the canal, an old man tied a mug with a rope and scooped up some water from the canal to drink. It was the first time he had drunk the water of the Zhanghe River in his life. People rushed to the canal and ran together with the flowing water. The mountains were full of laughter, and the people were full of joy. All the bitterness people had experienced became a long canal. All the sweat people had shed turned into rushing canal water. Weren't all the devotions and sacrifices for this special day?

续建支渠配套工程

在缺水、盼水的林县人眼里，红旗渠日夜流淌的是一渠粮、一渠油、一渠欢喜泪、一渠丰收酒、一渠哺育生命的乳汁……林县人时刻在盘算着如何最大限度地利用红旗渠水，让红旗渠发挥到最大效益。总干渠修成了，三条干渠也修成了，但这些都是"干"，还缺少"枝"，缺少毛细血管，还没有形成网。因此，必须乘胜前进，在一干渠、二干渠、三干渠上继续建设规划总长度177公里的41条支渠，还要相应建设斗、农、毛渠。

从一干渠红英汇流垂直等高线布置的红英干渠，自合涧公社向东，穿过小店公社、采桑公社直达东姚公社，也称"合（涧）东（姚）线"。数不清的男女，弯弯曲曲地摆在几十里的渠线上，每个村几乎都是全出动，就连上学的中学生，在星期天或假期也都参加了支渠修建。山岭的高处，是开采石头的匠人，他们用锤錾把一块块石头切成大小不一的豆腐块，抬到渠线上，砌成渠道。

渠道从小店村后山上经过，村里的人承建这段渠道。那天中午，伴随着收工的民工回村，隆隆的炮声炸响。炮声过后，人们发现有一个炮没炸响。出现了哑炮，必须排除，否则下午大伙儿没法上工。排除哑炮是炮手的职责，炮手韩普吉二话没说，拿起工具就往工地走，突然他被一个女人拉住了，随即从他手上夺下工具，扭头向哑炮快步走去。这个女人正是韩普吉的媳妇陈秀琴，她冒着生命危险向山上走去，聚集在村头的人们心都提到了嗓子眼。就在大家替陈秀琴担心的时候，最不希望发生的事情还是发生了。一声巨响之后，浓烟升腾，碎石狂飞，未等烟尘散尽，人们不约而同地向山上狂跑。他们在渠沟里找到了血肉模糊的陈秀琴，赶忙把她送到医院。经抢救，陈秀琴的生命保住了，但永远失

Continued Construction of Branch Canals

In the eyes of the people of Linxian County who had been short of water, what was flowing in the Hongqiqu Canal day and night was grain, oil, joyful tears, harvest wine, milk to feed life... The people of Linxian County were always considering how to make the most use of the water and maximize its benefits. The General Main Canal was completed, and so were the three main canals. But they were only "trunks" without "branches". The network was not formed. Therefore, it was necessary to build 41 branch canals with a total length of 177 kilometers on the First Main Canal, the Second Main Canal and the Third Main Canal, and then to construct distribution canals, field canals and field ditches accordingly.

The Hongying Main Canal flowed eastward from Hejian Commune, passing through Xiaodian Commune and Caisang Commune, to Dongyao Commune, also known as the "He-Dong Line" (from Hejian to Dongyao). Countless men and women were working along the canal line, dozens of miles long. Almost all the villagers were mobilized and even the middle school students participated in the construction on Sundays or holidays. On the mountain top, the stonemasons mined stones and then processed them with hammers into regular blocks, which were carried to the construction site for the branch canal.

The canal passed through the mountain behind Xiaodian Village, and the villagers were in charge of the construction of this section. One day at noon, as the workers returned to the village, the rumbling blasting sounded. After the blasting, it was found that one blast hole did not blow up. The failed blast hole must be eliminated, otherwise the people could not work in the afternoon. It was the blaster's duty to eliminate the failed blast hole. The blaster Han Puji did not hesitate to pick up a tool and go to the site. Suddenly he was stopped by a woman. She took the tool from his hand and walked to the site quickly. This woman was Han Puji's wife, Chen Xiuqin. She risked her own life and walked up the hill. The people gathered near the village, waiting very nervously. Just when everyone was worried about Chen Xiuqin, the worst thing happened. After a loud bang, the smoke rose and the stones flew in all directions. Before the smoke disappeared, the people ran wildly onto the mountain. They found Chen Xiuqin, who was bloody, in the ditch, and hurriedly sent her to the hospital. After the emergency

去了左手。朴实的农家男女不会讲爱情的甜言蜜语，却用行动诠释了对爱情的忠贞。

二干渠上的13支渠要从河湾村跨过粉红江，长155米、高10米、宽2.5米、8个拱券的河湾渡槽就成为工程建设的关键节点。渡槽建设中，向上运料就靠圆木或木板搭的马道。底层的马道最宽，随着槽墩升高，马道也呈之字型往上架高，越往上马道越窄，最高处仅有0.5米宽。槽墩底部用大石块砌筑，大部分石头需要四个人用两根杠子抬。砌到需搭第一层马道时，大部分就用一根杠子抬石头。

槽墩升高到起拱的高度，马道更窄，从下往上看，好像是悬在高空的独木桥。走马道向上抬石头，白天还得加倍小心，到了晚上就更加危险了。一天晚上，郎垒村的郭世杰和周成林用一根杠子往上抬一块约有四百斤重的大石头，两个人都鼓足勇气登上了马道架板，旁边有人当扶手。护到上层因架板、马道窄得容不下护杠人，只好撤离。抬杠子都是后面的指挥前面。在后面的郭世杰一手握杠，一手扶住杠上的石头，以防摇摆，他们相互配合，步调一致，万无一失地把大石头抬上了渡槽顶部。他们就这样干了一夜，顺利完成了当天的任务。

建设中的河湾渡槽
The Hewan Aqueduct under construction

treatment, Chen Xiuqin's life was saved, but she lost her left hand forever. The plain couple could not speak the sweet words of love, but their action interpreted the loyalty to love.

The 13th Branch Canal on the Second Main Canal would cross the Fenhong River at Hewan Village. The Hewan Aqueduct, which was 155 meters long, 10 meters high and 2.5 meters wide with 8 arches, became the key in the construction of the project. In the construction of the aqueduct, the transportation of the materials depended on round logs or wooden boardwalks. The bottom boardwalk was the widest. As the piers rose, the boardwalk was also elevated in a zigzag pattern and became narrower and narrower. The top boardwalk was only half a meter wide. The pier bottom was built with large stones, most of which required four people to lift with two poles. When the pier was built up to the first layer of boardwalk, most stones were carried with one pole by two people.

When the pier rose to the height of the arch, the boardwalk was even narrower and looked like a single-log bridge suspended overhead. Carrying stones on the boardwalk had to be careful even during the daytime and was more dangerous at night. One night, Guo Shijie and Zhou Chenglin from Langlei Village carried a large stone, nearly two hundred kilograms, with a pole. Both men took courage and climbed onto the boardwalk, with someone standing by as a handrail. The upper boardwalk was so narrow that the protectors had to withdraw. When a stone was carried with a pole by two men, the man behind gave directions. Guo Shijie at the back held the pole tightly with one hand and the stone with the other hand to prevent the swing. They cooperated and kept pace with each other, and carried the big stone to the top of the aqueduct safely. They worked for a whole night and successfully completed the task of the day.

郭世杰觉得两人抬石头风险太大，就独自往上背。他捡了一块约有100斤重的长石头要背，两个人费了很大劲才把石头给他抬到肩上。郭世杰一只手伸上去扣着石头，另一只手紧紧卡住腰，上到最高的独木板。迈步时，看脚下，起步时，向前看，走了十几步险道，终于把石头背到垒砌人员的面前。5300立方米的料石，就是这样靠人力一块块或抬或背地送上去的，可以说渡槽是用人的肩膀扛起来的。

红旗渠三干渠从曙光洞出来，分为南北两条支渠，向东北方向的三支渠来到了招军垴，隔一座低矮山梁——丁冶岭，与虎头山相望。渠道要跨过这个山坳，就要在这里建一座高16米、长550米、宽3.5米，共29孔的渡槽。

1969年4月2日渡槽开工后，没有石料、没有木料、没有抬筐、没有石灰，只有靠自己去寻找破解难题的方法。石料山上开，石灰就地烧，木材是群众把自家盖房用的木料拿来的，抬筐是到15公里外的深山里割回荆条自己动手编的，所用物料全靠自己生产。渡槽的地基基础软硬不一，有砂岩，有黏土，建设者们根据不同的岩层采取不同的方法。在岩石地基上按照设计的底宽5.4米的宽度，开出平整光洁的长条形墩基，再用料石平铺。在黏土上则深挖，将黏土夯实，然后用砂浆砌石。随着槽墩的节节升高，高空运料越来越难，需要使用吊车。这么大的渡槽，最少需要两台吊车，可是两台吊车每天仅燃油费和司机的生活费就要几百元，到渡槽完工时总共需要几万元，而整个渡槽总投资预算才38万元。这样做不划算，还得自己想办法。俗话说，吊桶打水——七上八下，民工们就是在七上八下的思虑中，从吊桶打水中得到启发，载高杆

Guo Shijie felt that it was too risky for two men to carry one stone together, and he began to work alone. He picked a stone about 50 kilograms, and two men helped him to lift the stone onto his shoulder with great effort. Guo Shijie buckled the stone with one hand and supported his waist with the other. He walked up to the highest wooden board. Watching his steps, he moved forward carefully. Finally, he carried the stone to the stonemason's side. In this way, 5,300 cubic meters of stones were sent by manpower to the site. In a sense, the aqueduct was erected by shoulders.

Flowing out of the Shuguang Tunnel, the Third Main Canal was divided into two branch canals, a northern one and a southern one. The third branch to the northeast direction arrived at a place named Zhaojunnao, facing the Hutou Mountain across a low ridge named Dingyeling. To cross the valley, the canal required a 29-hole aqueduct, 16 meters high, 550 meters long and 3.5 meters wide.

After the start of the aqueduct on April 2, 1969, there was no stone, no wood, no basket, and no lime. It relied on the builders themselves to solve all the problems. Stones were mined on the mountain and lime was processed on the spot. The villagers brought their wood prepared for their houses. Baskets were hand-made with canes, which were cut on the mountains 15 kilometers away. The materials used were all produced by themselves. The foundation of the aqueduct consisted of sandstone and clay, varying in hardness. The builders took different approaches depending on the rock formation. In sandstone, pier foundation 5.4 meters wide was excavated according to the design and then placed with stones. Where clay appeared, deep excavation was carried out, clay mixed with stones was compacted, and then wet masonry was built. As the piers rose, high-altitude transportation was becoming more and more difficult, requiring the use of a crane. Such a large aqueduct needed at least two cranes. However, the fuel cost of the two cranes and the living expenses of the operators were several hundred *yuan* per day, which would add up to tens of thousands of *yuan* when the aqueduct was completed. However, the total investment budget of the entire aqueduct was only 380,000 *yuan*. It was not cost-effective and they had to find a way. As the saying goes, water was fetched with 15 lifting buckets — 7 moving up and 8 moving down. The workers were inspired. They made cranes with lifting booms. In the

造土吊车，只不过吊桶打水的吊杆前端只有一桶水的重量，而土吊车的吊杆前端吊起的是500多公斤的物料。吊杆打水的后端一个人操作就可以很轻松地完成了，而土吊车却需要6个人拼命往下拉，一口气拉到位，中间不能有丝毫的松懈。吊桶打水不需要那么精准到位，土吊车吊送的物料必须精准地吊达指定的位置。8部土吊车造成了，在工地上一字排开，上下飞舞。在困难的日子里，这方生民齐心建起了这座渡槽。整个工程挖掘土石方0.69万立方米，砌石1.7万立方米，投工36万个，历经83天的苦战，于1969年6月25日竣工。渡槽像是切割天空的一道石青色的长链，粗犷中不乏细腻，冰冷中透着生命之暖。它又像一位英雄，以铁的手臂拉紧两座山，让渠水安全通过。

从1968年10月到1969年7月，林县人民斩断1004座山头，跨越850条沟壑，修建90多座渡槽，凿通70多个隧洞，完成了红旗渠配套工程。从1960年2月到1969年7月，林县人民奋斗了十年，每一步都如虹贯日、气

空中俯瞰曙光渡槽
A bird's-eye view of the Shuguang Aqueduct

case of the lifting boom to fetch water, the front end of the boom was only the weight of a bucket of water and the rear end of the boom could be easily operated by one person. But in the case of locally-made cranes, the front end of the boom was materials more than 500 kilograms and the rear end of the boom required 6 people to pull down with great effort in one breath. Fetching water with lifting buckets did not need to be so accurate, but hoisting materials with the locally-made crane must be accurately operated to the designated position. Eight locally-made cranes were produced and lined up on the construction site, hoisting goods up and down. In the difficult days, the local people worked together to build the aqueduct. For the construction of the aqueduct, 6,900 cubic meters of excavation and 17,000 cubic meters of masonry were carried out, and 360,000 man-days were used. After 83 days of hard work, it was completed on June 25, 1969. The aqueduct looked like a long chain across the sky, with no lack of exquisiteness in the rough and the warmth of life revealed in the cold. It was also like a hero who stretched his arms and grasped two mountains tightly to let the canal pass safely.

From October 1968 to July 1969, the people of Linxian County excavated 1,004 hills, crossed 850 gullies, built more than 90 aqueducts, cut through over 70 tunnels and completed the supporting project of the Hongqiqu Canal. From February 1960 to July 1969, the people of Linxian County struggled for ten years,

壮山河。30万人参与修建，81人牺牲，完全凭着一锤一钎，削平了1250座山头，凿通了211个隧洞，架设152座渡槽，总投资6865.64万元，挖土石方1818万立方米，硬是在太行山的悬崖峭壁上修成了一条全长1500公里的人工天河——红旗渠。有人计算过，如果把修建红旗渠所挖的土石方修成高2米、宽3米的墙，可从哈尔滨修到广州。这条人工天河，由总干渠到干渠，再由干渠分为支渠、斗渠、农渠、毛渠，终将连接而成一张巨大的水网，流到林县的一座座城镇、一个个村头、一方方田园，无声地滋润着岁月，编织着未来。

full of power and grandeur. 300,000 people participated in the construction, for which 81 people laid down their lives. They flattened 1,250 hills with their hands, excavated 211 tunnels and constructed 152 aqueducts, with a total investment of 68,656,400 *yuan* and excavation of 18,180,000 cubic meters. On the cliffs of the Taihang Mountains, they constructed a 1,500-kilometer-long man-made heavenly river, the Hongqiqu Canal. It was calculated that the earth and stone excavated for the construction of the Hongqiqu Canal could be built into a wall 2 meters high and 3 meters wide from Harbin to Guangzhou. The man-made heavenly river consisted of the General Main Canal, main canals, branch canals, distribution canals, field canals and field ditches, which formed a huge water network and flowed to towns, villages and fields in Linxian County, silently nourishing the years and weaving the future.

红旗渠带来的深刻变化

红旗渠引来幸福水,无疑为林县的发展增添了强大的引擎,不仅灌溉着土地,滋润着枯黄的禾苗,而且拓宽了发展路径和空间。

红旗渠独特的无调节河道自流引水,形成了罕见的渠道引水枢纽。它的通水,使全县有14个乡镇、410个行政村受益,60多万人口和3.7万头牲畜吃水有了可靠保障。伴着红旗渠水汩汩流淌,渠水所到之处的地下水得到了有效补给。很多村庄以前打井不见水,现在机井打出了水,大多数村庄都吃上了自来水。过去翻山越岭去挑水,今天红旗渠水从门前流过。

红旗渠水从门前流过
The water of the Hongqiqu Canal flows by the house

Profound Changes Brought about by the Hongqiqu Canal

The Hongqiqu Canal has brought water of happiness, which undoubtedly acts as a powerful engine to the development of Linxian County. It not only irrigates the land and nourishes the crops, but also broadens the path and space for development.

The unique artesian water diversion of the Hongqiqu Canal is a rare canal diversion hub. Its water supply has benefited 14 townships and 410 administrative villages in the county, and more than 600,000 people and 37,000 heads of livestock have access to reliable water. The water flowing in the Hongqiqu Canal has effectively replenished the groundwater along its path. In many villages, there used to be no water at all in wells excavated, but now the wells can provide water and most villages have access to tap water. In the past, people climbed up the mountains to fetch water; today the water of the Hongqiqu Canal flows in front of their gates.

红旗渠水使粮食增产得到保障，林县农业生产条件发生了变化。54万亩耕地得以灌溉，粮食产量逐年提高。红旗渠通水前林县粮食亩产只有几十公斤，通水后亩产达到四百多公斤。更令人惊喜的是，林县土地上开始种植水稻了。过去大多数林县人一辈子都不可能吃上一顿大米饭，而今自己种上了水稻，能吃上自己种的大米了，林县人的食物结构和饮食方式发生了明显变化，"糠菜半年粮"的时代一去不复返了。

在生存条件得到改变的同时，林县的发展条件也得到了根本改变，林县发展的一切因素都被激活了。

有了红旗渠，林县的种植业结构也在发生变化。种粮由过去以耐旱的秋作物为主，转变为夏秋并重，乃至演变为以夏季小麦作物为主。改过去单一的种植粮食作物为逐步种植黄花菜、药材、油菜等经济作物，农业的效益不断得到提升。

有了水，林业得到大发展。1500公里长渠沿线栽上了树，成为1500公里葱绿的林带。城乡道路两旁栽植了行道树，成为连接城乡的绿色通道。千年的荒山披上了绿装，万年的荒滩变成了果园。生态林、经济林同步发展，大地林网化，山区造梯田，呈现出"松柏林盖(山)顶、经济林缠(山)腰、用材林铺(山)底"的林茂粮丰的立体绿化景观。花椒、核桃、柿子、山楂、板栗等经济林的大面积种植，为林县人民创造了新的财富。林县被林业部命名为"全国经济林名、优、特商品生产基地"。

The water of the Hongqiqu Canal has ensured the increase of food supplies, and the agricultural production condition in Linxian County has changed greatly. The 36,000 hectares of cultivated land are irrigated and the grain output increases year by year. Before the Hongqiqu Canal was put into operation, the grain yield per hectare was only hundreds of kilograms in Linxian County, and now the yield per hectare has reached more than 6,000 kilograms. More surprisingly, rice has started to be planted on the land of Linxian County. In the past, most people in Linxian County could not eat a single meal of rice in their lifetime. Now they grow rice themselves and can eat their own rice. The food structure and diet style of the people of Linxian County have changed significantly, and the days that "chaffs and potherbs are eaten as food for half a year" are gone forever.

While the living conditions are changed, the development conditions in Linxian County have also been fundamentally changed, and all the elements for the development of Linxian County have been activated.

With the Hongqiqu Canal, the planting structure of Linxian County is also changing. In the past, drought-tolerant autumn crops were mainly planted, but now equal attention is paid to summer and autumn crops, and even summer wheat evolves into the main crop. Instead of only planting food crops in the past, people gradually plant cash crops, such as daylilies, herbs and oilseed rape, and the agricultural benefits have been constantly improved.

With water, forestry has been developed greatly. Trees are planted along the 1,500-kilometer-long canal line, creating a green forest belt. Trees are planted on both sides of urban and rural roads, which become green passages connecting urban and rural areas. Barren mountains are covered with green trees, and wastelands are turned into orchards. Ecological forests and economic forests are developing synchronously. The land is forested and the mountains are transformed into terraces. Thus the three-dimensional green landscape presents a picture of the pine and cypress forest covering the top, the economic forest surrounding the mountainside and the timber forest spreading over the foot of the maintains. The large-scale planting of economic forests such as wild pepper, walnut, persimmon, haw and chestnut has created new wealth for the people of Linxian County. Linxian County is named by the Ministry of Forestry as the "Famous, Excellent, Special Commodity Production Base of the National Economic Forest". The

全县森林覆盖率达到40%。林业的发展增加了群众收入,林县的生态环境也得到了根本改善。

有了水,发展畜牧养殖业就有了条件。林县人民利用大量的水库、池塘,在太行山上养鱼、养鸭、养鹅,谱写了一曲"太行渔歌",从此水产品也出现在林县人民的餐桌上了。奶牛场、养猪场、养兔场、养鸡场、养羊场等大型养殖场和养殖基地建起来了,林县的农业产业结构不断得到优化。

红旗渠的建设带来了林县小水电的大发展。全县利用水力资源,在县、乡、村建起108处大中小型水电站,装机172台,总容量22710千瓦,年发电5600万千瓦时。小水电的发展,为林县的工农业发展提供了强劲动力,为农村带来现代化的气息。粮食加工告别了传统的碾子和磨盘,电灯代替油灯,照亮了古老山村的夜晚,也使林县人民看到了光明。

太行渔歌
Taihang fishermen's songs

county's forest coverage rate reached 40%. The development of forestry has increased the income of the local people, and the ecological environment of Linxian County has also been fundamentally improved.

With water, it is possible to develop livestock breeding and cultivation. The people of Linxian County use a large number of reservoirs and ponds to raise fish, ducks and geese on the Taihang Mountains, and since then, the aquatic products are often seen on the dining tables of the people of Linxian County. Large-scale livestock farms and breeding bases such as dairy farms, pig farms, rabbit warrens, henneries and sheep farms are established. The agricultural production structure of Linxian County has been continuously optimized.

The construction of the Hongqiqu Canal has brought the great development of small hydropower in the county. The whole county has used the water resources to build 108 hydropower stations of different sizes in the county, townships and villages, and has installed 172 hydroelectric generators, with a total capacity of 22,710 kilowatts and an annual power generation of 56 million kilowatt hours. The development of small hydropower stations has provided a strong driving force for the development of industry and agriculture in Linxian County, bringing a modern atmosphere to the countryside. The grain processing no longer relies on the traditional stone rollers and millstones. The electric lights have replaced the oil lamps, illuminating the nights of the ancient mountain villages and making the people of Linxian County see the bright future.

有了红旗渠，林县的工业发展有了活力。除为支援红旗渠工程建设而兴建的水泥厂、机械修配厂、小煤矿外，又建起了化肥厂、小拖拉机厂、粮食加工厂，各乡镇也都建起了农机修造厂。这些小企业的兴建，为全县未来的工业化发展奠定了基础。

有了红旗渠，林县的交通、邮电事业也得到发展。未修渠，先修路，先通邮电，红旗渠修到哪里，道路就通到哪里，邮电就跟到哪里。红旗渠修成后，人们又利用修渠的弃渣修建乡村道路。随着红旗渠走向全国，对参观红旗渠的线路拓宽铺油，由乡间土路改造为柏油路170多公里。这在20世纪70年代初的中国县级行政区的道路建设上，是极其少见的。邮电线路也随着红旗渠工程的延伸而延伸，随着红旗渠的竣工而逐步完善。红旗渠通水之日起，林县实现了村村通电话、广播。

红旗渠的建成使林县由封闭落后的地区变为对外开放的典型地区。1973年，国务院下发文件，批准林县为"全国对外开放单位"。从1970到1980年先后有世界上119个国家和地区的11000名外宾和我国香港、澳门的众多同胞来林县参观红旗渠。国内各地有组织地来林县参观红旗渠的人数达162.4万。可以说，红旗渠的建设是林县对外开放和发展旅游的发端。

With the Hongqiqu Canal, the industrial development of Linxian County has gained vitality. In addition to the cement plants, mechanical repairing plants and small coal mines built to support the construction of the Hongqiqu Canal, chemical fertilizer plants, small tractor factories and grain processing factories have been set up, and agricultural machinery repair factories have also been established in various villages and towns. The establishment of these small enterprises has laid the foundation for the future industrialization of the county.

With the Hongqiqu Canal, the transportation and the posts and telecommunications in Linxian County have also developed accordingly. Before the construction of the canals, roads should be built and post and telecommunications should be put into operation first. Where the Hongqiqu Canal went, roads and post and telecommunications went in advance. After the completion of the Hongqiqu Canal, people used the waste excavated material to build rural roads. As the Hongqiqu Canal became well-known all over China, the country road to the Hongqiqu Canal was widened and transformed into an asphalt pavement of more than 170 kilometers. This was extremely rare in the road construction of China's county-level administrative regions in the early 1970s. The post and telecommunications routes were also extended with the extension of the Hongqiqu Canal and improved gradually with the completion of the Hongqiqu Canal. Since the day the Hongqiqu Canal was put into use, all villages in Linxian County have obtained access to telephones and broadcasting.

The completion of the Hongqiqu Canal has turned Linxian County from a closed and backward area into a typical area open to the outside world. In 1973, the State Council issued a document approving Linxian County as a national organization open to the outside world. From 1970 to 1980, 11,000 foreign guests from 119 countries and regions and a lot compatriots from Hong Kong and Macao came to Linxian County to visit the Hongqiqu Canal. The number of organized visitors coming to Linxian County to visit the Hongqiqu Canal from all over the country reached 1.624 million. It means that the construction of the Hongqiqu Canal is the beginning of the opening up and the development of tourism in Linxian County.

Mr. DeMann from the United Nations visited the Hongqiqu Canal in May 1972. At the symposium after his visit, Mr. DeMann commented with emotion,

外宾参观红旗渠
Foreign guests visit the Hongqiqu Canal

1972年5月，在联合国工作的迪曼先生参观了红旗渠。在参观红旗渠后的座谈会上，迪曼先生感慨地说："我到过世界上许多国家，参观过许多闻名于世的伟大建筑。号称世界七大奇迹的古代建筑中，除金字塔外，其他六大奇迹已因地震、火灾和人为破坏等原因而毁坏。我认真参观过埃及的金字塔，那确实了不起，但它只是埋葬法老等人的陵墓，而红旗渠是造福人民的，所以我要说，参观了红旗渠，有必要更改历史的说法，世界上有七大奇迹不对，红旗渠应列为第八大奇迹。它不仅是技术上的成功和突破，而且是政治上的意志和战胜。"

1972年12月，几内亚总理兰萨纳·贝阿沃吉在参观红旗渠时由衷地感叹："红旗渠给我们留下了深刻的印象，的确是了不起的工程。"

1974年2月，赞比亚总统肯尼斯·戴维·卡翁达参观红旗渠后讲道："感谢毛主席、周总理给我们安排了这样好的参观项目，我建议所有发展中国家，也就是第三世界，都来这里学习。"

"I have visited many countries and lots of famous great buildings in the world. Among the ancient buildings known as the Seven Wonders of the World, six of them have been destroyed due to earthquakes, fires and human damage except for the pyramids of Egypt which I've also visited. They are amazing, but they are just mausoleums of pharaohs. However, the Hongqiqu Canal benefits people. So I think we need to change the historical saying after visiting the Canal. It is wrong to say there are seven wonders in the world, as the Hongqiqu Canal should be listed as the eighth, which is not only a technical success and breakthrough, but also a political will and victory."

When visiting the Hongqiqu Canal in December 1972, Guinean Prime Minister Lansana Baiawoji sincerely said, "Hongqiqu Canal deeply impressed us. It is indeed a great project."

In February 1974, the President of Zambia, Kenneth David Kaunda, said after his visit to the Canal, "Thank Chairman Mao and Premier Zhou for arranging such a good visit. I suggest that people from all developing countries, that is, the third world, come here to have a look."

Deng Xiaoping, then Vice Premier of the State Council, led a delegation of Chinese government to attend the sixth special session of the United Nations

1974年4月，时任国务院副总理的邓小平率中国政府代表团出席联合国第六次特别会议，随团带去了10部介绍新中国建设成就的电影片，在联合国总部放映。第一部就是《红旗渠》，引起媒体高度关注。美联社发文称："红旗渠的人工修建，是毛泽东意志在红色中国的典范，看后令世界震惊！"

1974年5月，塞内加尔新闻部部长阿萨内·恩迪亚耶参观红旗渠时说："中国的长城在世界上很有名，毛主席领导的两万五千里长征也很有名，今天的红旗渠同样闻名于世界。"

1974年6月，加纳农业部部长内纳斯科在红旗渠上深有感触地说："红旗渠这样的工程，不亲眼看，难以相信；亲眼看了，又很难找到恰当的语言来表达。"

1977年6月，索马里共和国副总统伊斯梅尔·阿里·阿布尔卡参观红旗渠后盛赞："林县人民是改造大自然的主人，是世界人民学习的榜样，红旗渠是当代世界的奇迹。"

1978年4月，联合国水利考察组考察红旗渠后赞扬说："世界上任何其他国家都不会看到这种艰巨的石工建筑。"

1979年8月，马耳他共和国议会议长尔西登·阿求斯参观红旗渠时激动地说："看了红旗渠，我回去怎么说？想来想去只有说，你们都去看看。"

太行岿然，长渠不息。红旗渠的建设者开启了一条创造历史的精神航道，塑造了中华民族继往开来的精神丰碑，也成为中华民族向世界展示自己性格的一张名片，提供了一个中国读本。时至今日，一批批的外国政要、各界人士来到红旗渠浏览这张名片，翻阅这部中国故事读本，仍然会情不自禁地给予由衷的肯定和高度评价。

in April 1974. He brought 10 films about the achievements of new China, which were shown at the headquarters of the United Nations. The first one was a documentary of the Hongqiqu Canal, which attracted great attention of the media. The Associated Press wrote "The man-made Hongqiqu canal is the outstanding embodiment of Chairman Mao Zedong's will in Red China, which shocked the world."

Asane Ndiaye, Minister of the Ministry of Public Information of Senegal, said when visiting the Hongqiqu Canal in May 1974, "The Great Wall of China is quite famous in the world, and the Long March of 25000 li led by Chairman Mao is also famous, so it is with nowadays' Hongqiqu Canal."

In June 1974, Ghana's Minister of Agriculture, Nenasco, said with deep feelings on the Hongqiqu Canal, "It's hard to believe such a project as the Hongqiqu Canal without seeing it with your own eyes; it's also hard to find proper words to express it after seeing it with your own eyes."

Ismail Ali Abulka, Vice President of the Republic of Somalia, paid a visit to the Hongqiqu Canal in June 1977 and spoke highly of the local people and the project, "The people of Linxian County are the masters of transforming the nature and the role model of other peoples. The Canal is a miracle of the contemporary world."

"This kind of stonework can not be seen in any other country in the world," the Water Resources Investigation Team Members of UN commented after a visit in April 1978.

In August 1979, the President of the Parliament of the Republic of Malta, Ershiden Atus, visited the Canal and said excitedly, "What will I say when I go back after visiting the Hongqiqu Canal? I can only tell them that you have to go there and have a look."

As Taihang Mountain has been standing there stilland long, the canal has been flowing and will flow endlessly. The Hongqiqu canal has not only been a project to solve the problem of much needed water in Lin county, but also has been a monument to record the national character. Many foreign visitors, including top leaders and people from all walks of life, have come a long way to visit the canal. Once when they are there, they are always amazed by the spectacular project.

2004年11月，在上海举办的红旗渠精神展上，来自瑞士的马科斯·迈尔先生，借来上海参加一个国际会议之机参观了红旗渠精神展，他感慨地说："瑞士和中国，以及全世界的所有国家都应该携起手来，更好地保护水资源，保护水环境，这是红旗渠告诉我们的。红旗渠就是一本最生动的水资源保护教科书。"

2012年9月，在林州举办的国际和平日仪式上，曾经担任过联合国环境项目负责人的诺尔·布朗博士讲道："我对红旗渠的故事及其象征的精神早有耳闻，在'红旗渠精神'的故乡举办国际和平日活动，可以告诉世界，精神能够为人类提供战胜一切困难的力量。"

2015年10月，坦桑尼亚总统府官员利蓬巴在参观红旗渠时动情地说："红旗渠应该作为世界文化遗产，与世界人民共享。"

2017年5月，美国密歇根大学环境与可持续发展学院副教授、密歇根大学可持续发展案列中心主任Rebecca Hardin在考察红旗渠后讲道："我们了解了红旗渠，了解了在修建红旗渠过程中修建者的艰难困苦，这种精神是没有国界的。这让我想起了我的故乡美国在遭受大萧条的时候，我的祖辈们那时候特别的恐惧，但是他们仍然为我们做出了一些贡献，为我们后来的发展奠定了一定的基础，我们正在享受他们的劳动成果。我不知道中国是否还有像红旗渠这样不单靠技术完成的伟大工程，他们（红旗渠建设者）度过了那样漫长的修渠岁月，为以后的发展奠定了基础。"

2018年5月，埃塞俄比亚驻华大使馆公使衔参赞尼古斯·科布德参观红旗渠后表示："红旗渠精神将为包括埃塞在内的广大发展中国家的发展提供精神力量，埃塞人民要好好学习红旗渠精神，把自己的国家建设好、发展好"。

2019年7月，突尼斯共和国外交顾问Adel Ben Abdallah参观红旗渠后

In November 2004, Mr. Marcos Mayer from Switzerland took the chance of attending an international conference in Shanghai to visit the exhibition of the Hongqiqu Canal Spirit. "Switzerland and China, as well as all other countries in the world, should work together to better protect water resources and water environment, which is what the Hongqiqu Canal teaches us," he said with emotion, "it is one of the most vivid textbooks on water resources protection."

In September 2012, at the ceremony of International Peace Day held in Linzhou (the present name of Linxian County), Dr. Noel Brown, who once served as the Head of the United Nations Environment Program, said, "I've heard the story of the Canal and its symbolic spirit for a long time. By holding the International Peace Day in the hometown of the Hongqiqu Canal spirit, we can tell the world that the spirit can give us strength to overcome all difficulties."

In October 2015, the official of the Tanzanian presidential office, Lipumba, said passionately when visiting the canal, "It should be considered as a world cultural heritage and shared with other peoples of the world."

In May 2017, Rebecca Hardin, Associate Professor of the Association of Environment and Sustainable Development of the University of Michigan and Director of the Case Center of Sustainable Development Program of the University, remarked after his visit, "We have learned about the Hongqiqu Canal and the difficulties of its builders. This spirit has no national boundaries, which reminds me of what happened in the Great Depression in the US. My forefathers were very scared at that time, but they still made some contributions for us and laid a foundation for our later development. Now we are enjoying the fruits of their labor. I wonder if there are other great projects like Hongqiqu Canal in China, which is not completed by technology alone. The builders of the project spent such a long and hard time in the construction, laying a foundation for future development."

In May 2018, after visiting the Hongqqu canal, Mr. Negus Kebede Kassaw, Minister counsellor of the Ethiopian Embassy in China, said, "the construction of this great project in China will surely inspire people of other developing nations. The Ethiopians should learn from the Chinese people, working hard for a better and richer country".

In July 2019, Adel Ben Abdallah, the Diplomatic Adviser of the Republic of

留言:"如果有一幅能体现伟大中国人民真实价值的圣象,在我看来,红旗渠是当之无愧的,它的寓意值得许多民族思考。"

2019年9月,俄罗斯联邦共产党中央书记、列宁共产主义青年团中央第一书记弗拉基米尔·伊萨科夫参观红旗渠后表示:"红旗渠是中国人民勤劳勇敢的结果,更是中华民族精神的象征。这些将载入史册,影响中国甚至世界"。

修建红旗渠,林县人民增长了胆略和才智,培养了一大批人才。建渠十年,培养各类人才7747人,其中工程师27名,技术员560名。在当时教育、科技相对落后的条件下,能培养出这么多人才,是极其难得的,他们也是林县非常宝贵的资源。

凝聚着林县人民心血的红旗渠,彻底改变了林县的历史,改变了林县人民的命运。林县,这个在中华大地上原本平常的一个地方,从此迈开了走向全国、走向世界的坚强步伐。

这条人工天河作为一种状态、一种可以感知而又难以触摸的精神,郑重地传承给后人。

红旗渠承载着林州人的梦想,改变生活,昭示未来。

Tunisia, left a message after visiting the Canal, "If there is a holy image that can reflect the true value of the great Chinese people, in my opinion, Hongqiqu Canal deserves it. Its implication is worth thinking for many other nationalities."

In September 2019, Vladimir Isakov, Secretary of the Central Committee of the Communist Party of the Russian Federation and first Secretary of the Central Committee of Lenin Communist Youth League, said after visiting the project, "the Hongqiqu canal is the fruit of the hard work and bravery of the Chinese people, and it is also a symbol of the national character. It will be recorded in history and affects China as well as the world."

Through the construction of the Hongqiqu Canal, the people of Linxian County have increased their courage and wisdom and have trained a large number of talents. In the ten years of the construction of the Canal, 7,747 talents of various types were cultivated, including 27 engineers and 560 technicians. Under the conditions of relatively backward education and technology at that time, it was extremely rare to be able to cultivate so many talents. They were also very valuable resources in Linxian County.

The Hongqiqu Canal, which embodies the painstaking efforts of the people of Linxian County, has completely changed the history of Linxian County and the destiny of the people of Linxian county. Linxian County, originally a common place in China, has since taken a strong step towards the whole country and the whole world.

This man-made heavenly river, as a state and a spirit that can be felt but not touched, is solemnly passed on to future generations.

The Hongqiqu Canal carries the dreams of the people of Linzhou, changes their lives and indicates their future.

附录
Appendix

中国历史年代简表
A Brief Chronology of Chinese History

五帝时代 Period of the Five Legendary Rulers c. 2600 BC~c. 20	黄帝 Huangdi (Yellow Emperor)	
	颛顼 Zhuanxu	
	帝喾 Diku (Emperor Ku)	
	（唐）尧 Yao	
	（虞）舜 Shun	
夏 Xia Dynasty	c. 2070 BC~ c. 1600 BC	
商 Shang Dynasty	c. 1600 BC~ c. 1046 BC	
西周 Western Zhou Dynasty	c. 1046 BC~ c. 771 BC	
东周 Eastern Zhou Dynasty 770 BC~256 BC	春秋 Spring and Autumn Period	770 BC~476BC
	战国 Warring States Period	475 BC~221 BC
秦 Qin Dynasty	221 BC~206 BC	
汉 Han Dynasty 206 BC~220 AD	西汉 Western Han	206 BC~25 AD
	东汉 Eastern Han	25~220
三国 Three Kingdoms 220~280	魏 Wei	220~265
	蜀汉 Shu Han	221~263
	吴 Wu	222~280
晋 Jin Dynasty 265~420	西晋 Western Jin	265~317
	东晋 Eastern Jin	317~420

续表 Continued Table

南北朝 Southern and Northern Dynasties 420~589	南朝 Southern Dynasties	宋 Song	420~479
		齐 Qi	479~502
		梁 Liang	502~557
		陈 Chen	557~589
	北朝 Northern Dynasties	北魏 Northern Wei	386~534
		东魏 Eastern Wei	534~550
		北齐 Northern Qi	550~577
		西魏 Western Wei	535~556
		北周 Northern Zhou	557~581
隋 Sui Dynasty		581~618	
唐 Tang Dynasty		618~907	
五代十国 Five Dynasties and Ten States	五代 Five Dynasties 907~960	后梁 Later Liang	907~923
		后唐 Later Tang	923~936
		后晋 Later Jin	936~947
		后汉 Later Han	947~950
		后周 Later Zhou	951~960
	十国 Ten States 902-979	北汉 Northern Han	951~979
		吴 Wu	902~937
		吴越 Wuyue	907~978
		闽 Min	909~945
		南汉 Southern Han	917~971
		荆南（又称"南平"）Jingnan (Nanping)	924~963
		楚 Chu	927~951
		南唐 Southern Tang	937~975
		前蜀 Former Shu	907~925
		后蜀 Later Shu	934~965

续表 Continued Table

宋 Song Dynasty 960~1279	北宋 Northern Song	960~1127
	南宋 Southern Song	1127~1279
辽 Liao (契丹 Qidan/Khitan)	907~1125	
金 Jin	1115~1234	
西夏 Xixia (Tangut)	1038~1227	
元 Yuan Dynasty	1206~1368	
明 Ming Dynasty	1368~1644	
清 Qing Dynasty	1616~1911	
中华民国 Republic of China	1912~1949	
中华人民共和国 People's Republic of China	1949~